D1117345

So, you're unique!

What's your point?

So, you're unique!

What's your point?

Mels Carbonell, Ph.D.

Uniquely You[TM] Resources
PO Box 490
Blue Ridge, GA 30513
Phone: (706) 492-5490
E-mail: drmels@myuy.com
Web site: www.myuy.com

So, you're unique!
What's your point?

Dedicated to —

Roger Barnett, President of the Shaklee Corporation and my entire Shaklee family who through their examples and passions have encouraged me to be more health conscious and committed to helping others achieve their wellness and financial goals.

If you would like to know more about Shaklee's products, go to ***www.shaklee.com*** or to find a distributor near you, go to ***www.shaklee.net*** and click on ***Find a Distributor.***

To hear a special brief recorded message from Roger Barnett, phone 1-925-924-3333.

ISBN 1-888846-01-1

First Edition

Contents

Introduction

So, you're unique! — If you do not think so, then this book may not be for you. If you possibly see yourself as naturally endowed to succeed in life, then read on. Fulfilling your purpose involves understanding not only the *why*, but also the *how* you are wired.

What's your point? — because there is so much to learn about *why* and *how* people do what they do! It necessitates knowing yourself — what makes you tick and what ticks you off. It also requires your understanding of others. Learning how to relate wisely to people is vital to fulfilling your purpose!

Understanding Human Behavior Science is imperative for success in business and life. This learning process begins by identifying the unique personality types everyone has and how they relate in all walks of life. You will then learn how to successfully live and work more effectively with people. That is a definite point you should never ignore.

Discovering and developing the potential within you is a life long journey. Your personality plays an important role as you grow in experience and wisdom. You were designed with a unique framework to become a great leader.

There is no single personality type that is better than the others for becoming a successful business person. No one has a "bad" personality. It is what you do with your personality that really matters.

The biggest challenges business people and leaders often face are the "people problems."

Most conflicts are caused by personality clashes. Each individual acts, feels and thinks according to his or her temperament. Learning how unique people are *IS THE POINT!*

Leaders, especially, need to discover and understand the

different types of personalities. Recognizing what drives people can be very enlightening. This book focuses on the four temperament DISC Model of Human Behavior. It is a tool to drive home the point of why you bog down or overcome the obstacles of life and business.

Hopefully this information will result in better attitudes, improved relationships and more effective results for you. Identifying your personality and how you tend to live and work with others can be the beginning of a new way of solving your "people-problems."

To help you identify your specific personality type there should be a sticker with a *FREE* code on the inside front cover of this book. Go on the internet to *www.uniquelyyou.NET* and click on "For Professionals / Leaders" photo / link. Then click on "Create Account," enter the necessary information, and then add your code in the *Quick Start* boxes near the bottom of the right column to complete your profile.

Identifying and understanding your temperament and motivations can make the difference between your success or failure, especially as a leader and business person. Learning how to improve your life and leadership skills is a good *point* to start your journey toward becoming all that you were meant to be.

Personal Note

I am writing this Preface with serious apprehension. There is a part of me that is very spiritual and wants to help everyone, whether they believe as I do or not.

Yet, this book is for professionals and leaders regardless of their faith. The truths and principles I write about work for people of deep faith and for people with no faith. I personally believe that life is better with faith in God, but I acknowledge that no matter what you believe about the Creator, you can succeed in business.

I was actually raised an atheist. My father became a communist after coming to the US in 1928. He was even arrested and tried for "Un-American Activities" by Joseph McCarthy in 1954. I was only ten years old and did not really understand all that was happening.

My father was formally very religious as he grew up in Spain before immigrating to Cuba. He won a baseball contest in his early 20's and went to New York where he played baseball. Somehow, while in America he turned off to "churchianity" and "religianity."

He later became a spy for Fidel Castro and an informant for the F.B.I. His F.B.I. file is over 7,000 pages long. He also spent a year and a half imprisoned in Cuba to prove to the F.B.I. he could help them.

Capitalism and Communism

He was a wonderful father, but had "unique" ideas about capitalism and communism. I was in high school and college while most of his spying activity was happening. I was satisfied in my similar unbelief. I was content in believing that I was a product of chance and that there was no intelligent designer.

A neighborhood friend, Bud Tickle, invited me to a youth meeting. He was smarter than I, a better athlete, better looking, and made better grades than I. He was everything I thought

religious people were not supposed to be. I imagined every believer in God was an ignorant, anemic social reject.

I confess that I only went to the youth meeting for the fun and
because I saw a brown-haired, blue-eyed bombshell. I felt "led of
the Lord" to keep going back. I really was not interested in theolo-
gy. My motives were purely selfish, but as I continued to attend the
youth meetings, I began to debate and question my friend's faith.

As it turned out, I became a believer in the Holy Scriptures and
its message. I now want to be the best Christian I can be and never
compromise my faith. I also try not to be offensive or pushy. I
respect everyone's right to believe what he or she wants. But I must
confess that my passion is ministering to others so they too will
believe.

I decided to write this book from a secular perspective as a
benefit to all my unbelieving friends and clients. I sincerely desire
that they will find the same faith I have found, but I respect their
right to refuse it.

I also want to make clear that there is a big difference between
"churchianity" and Christianity, plus a big difference between
having a "religion" and having a "relationship with God by faith in
Christ as Savior."

You were constantly on my mind as I wrote this book, whether
you have a personal faith in God or not. I want to seriously help
you improve the quality of your life, your relationship with your
family, and your job performance.

Regardless of who you are, you can become just as successful
in business as anyone else. I sincerely pray that this book will be a
blessing and benefit to you.

Mels Carbonell, Ph.D.

Point #1

You ARE unique!

Just like no two snow flakes are alike, no two humans are exactly the same. Even identical twins have their differences.

Believe it or not, cloning animals has also proven how two cloned creatures are unique in themselves. Cloned sheep may be exact replicas according to their DNA, but they will still develop their own personalities and behave differently.

If the unfortunate day ever comes when humans are cloned, we will still see how cloned individuals will act, think, and feel independent of their cloned brother or sister.

Your uniqueness is primarily determined by your personality. You are unique because of how and why you do things. Your temperament often determines your behavior, which in turn makes you unique.

Everyone is also divinely designed! As a matter of fact, you are a gifted individual! You were created in your mother's womb with a natural "bent" of thinking, feeling, and acting that is unique.

Each of us has a distinctive personality that makes us special. Unfortunately, this does not include only good characteristics. We also need to learn how to guard our "strengths" and "uniqueness," especially when we are relating to others.

Understanding "what makes you tick" (your personality — the Uniquely You), is central to understanding why we have problems with people. Misunderstandings lead to clashes. Conflicts obviously hinder our effectiveness as mates, parents, and business people.

The word "discord" illustrates this best. The prefix "dis" is defined in the dictionary as "the Greek god of the underworld," while the word "cord" denotes the element that binds people or things together. Discord therefore divides and destroys relationships and success in life.

Understanding Our Motivations

Solving our "people problems" involves understanding our motivations. The Science of Human Behavior can explain our motivations. Why people do what they do is extremely interesting to most people. Humankind's varied behavior makes studying personality types most fascinating.

There is nothing more intriguing than discovering a person's motivations. Daily human drama revolves around the reasons for, and results of, our actions. Unlocking the mystery of motivation and behavior is the key to understanding people.

Comprehending personalities is what the Science of Human Behavior is all about. In order to live, work, and play in a healthy and happy environment, we must understand why people do what they do. Being able to read people makes life exciting and enjoyable.

Yet it frequently appears that "people" present life's biggest problems. Perhaps you have said, "Life would be great if it weren't for people!" It is a humorous, but sad commentary on how we often view one another.

One of our greatest challenges is learning how to relate to others — digging out of our people-pitfalls — becoming "people smart". In other words, it is learning how to be effective with people. Plain and simple, it is becoming *personality wise*.

Psychology and Human Behavior Science

The Science of Human Behavior is the study of our natural and predictable patterns of behavior. It focuses on the emotions of normal people. It differs from the Science of Psychology in that Psychology deals more deeply with abnormal behavior, while Human Behavior Science deals with normal responses and actions.

Basically, psychologists and psychiatrists specialize in helping the 10% of people who do what they do for abnormal reasons — a chemical imbalance, a "short-circuit," or perhaps a rebellion in the person's life. Human Behavior Scientists explain the reasons and actions of the other 90% of people who do what they do for natural and normal reasons.

This does not mean normal people will not do abnormal things. Everyone is capable of abnormal behavior, but what most normal people do can be explained by understanding their personalities.

This book is intended to help people with normal emotional challenges. Those with abnormal behavior are encouraged to seek qualified professionals who may be able to help them.

It is not coincidental that Mark H. McCormack began his best-selling book, *What They Don't Teach You at the Harvard Business School*, with the chapter "Reading People."

He obviously felt that one of America's most respected business schools makes a great omission — failing to teach how to become *people smart.*

Mastering the ability to read people can be equated to reading the news, watching the weather forecasts, or listening to financial reports in order to speculate the future. We must equip ourselves with the necessary information in order to make solid judgments in the present and sound predictions for the future in our relationships with others.

A Big Mistake

Steven Brown, the author of *13 Fatal Errors Managers Make,* also views the subject of people effectiveness as extremely important. *Fatal Error #5 is — "Trying To Manage Everyone The Same Way."* Knowing how to deal with people according to their temperaments is paramount in relationships of all types, not just managerial-oriented ones.

Understanding personalities is especially vital to surviving in the business world. We should also not underestimate its importance in avoiding bad marriages and family frustrations. Because divisions and disharmony are a fact of life, we need more than religious platitudes and "grin and bear it" attitudes to help us deal with these sticky situations.

The Science of Motivation focuses on the reasons we feel and respond the way we do. Just as the science of biology reveals the classifications of biological life — *genera, species, phyla, and kingdom* — so the Science of Human Behavior reveals there are predictable responses to, as well as the feelings produced by, various situations.

There is a definite myth about motivation. It is a mistake to think we can motivate others, like coaches who decide a stimulating pep talk is needed to win the game, teachers who try to persuade students to do better by insulting them, or parents who constantly restrict their children hoping to force them to improve their grades. These tactics may motivate some, but not most.

Have you ever said, "I wish my child was motivated," or "If that person was only motivated to ...!"? The truth is we can not motivate anyone to do anything they do not want to do. People do what they do because of their own reasons, not ours. We can try to manipulate and intimidate (which is wrong), but we can not motivate them.

Manipulation and intimidation often backfire. Using outside force to get people to do things can boomerang back to hurt and haunt us. All true motivation is intrinsic; it comes from within. People are motivated by their own feelings and for their own reasons.

Everyone is motivated, whether they take action in a particular situation or not. Some employees are motivated to work hard, while others are not motivated to study. The decision to act or not act is driven by the will of the individual. To say some people are not motivated because they do not take some sort of action is incorrect.

Motivation is not the ability to scream until people respond. It is not pep talks just before the big game. Motivation takes root and becomes personalized before we ever go into action. It begins with our personalities — why we do what we do. **The point is to create the climate and environment that makes people want to do what they should do.**

Comprehending the reality of personalities and their dynamic differences will greatly affect our lives. Our personalities are the unique ways we think, feel, and act — the way we were wired to respond.

There Are No Bad Personalities

Someone is probably thinking, "But you haven't met my mother-in-law" or "You don't know my boss." Perhaps they can be terrible. However, it is not a rotten personality, but rather how they use their personality that makes them behave so poorly. I believe we receive our personalities from our Creator, and we are molded and made into the people we become through our parents and peers as we grow into adolescence.

Even though the way we feel and think has definitely been influenced by our past, it does not have to control us. Happiness is a choice. We can allow our emotions to control us or we can choose to control our responses.

Keep in mind, we are discussing the emotions of normal people. We are not looking at abnormal behavior — those neurotic and psychotic personalities that come from an unfortunate short-circuit, chemical imbalance, or just plain rebellious life-styles that results in tragedies.

Ninety percent of the people we work with have normal emotional challenges. Everyone experiences simple to serious conflicts. By understanding the predictable patterns of behavior, we can avoid most clashes. We can also become more tolerant of differing personalities. Our goal should be to gain insights into the normal drives and passions of people.

Someone said, "Most relationships don't end due to sudden blowouts, but because of slow leaks." It is those slow leaks of misunderstandings, misreadings, and misgivings that destroy our relationships.

Our personalities should never be excuses for poor behavior. If you ever hit someone with a bat, you can not blame the bat. The problem was caused by your anger being out of control, not the bat.

Solving the mystery of motivation involves understanding the drives and passions of why people do what they do. Identifying personality types is critical to solving the "people puzzle."

This is a point that can not be over-emphasized. Missing this point can result in losing life's greatest challenges. Getting the point will increase your effectiveness and overall success in life.

Discovering Natural Motivations

We receive the skeleton of our personalities at conception. Many people believe we are divinely and genetically designed as distinct individuals for a purpose. Our parents and past experiences (our environment growing up) also often influenced us or, better yet, "developed" us into the persons we are today.

This is why the environment of our early childhood is extremely important. It influences our personality and the way we view others and ourselves. Nature and nurturing (early childhood development) both mold and shape us. When we are younger, we do not have the knowledge needed to deal properly with our hurts and disappointments, as well as our achievements and victories. However, we do have a choice as we grow older.

When a problem arises, one type of behavior may be perfectly natural, while the other is not. One comes easy, the other does not. Reacting from a human standpoint may seem right, but from another perspective it may not be appropriate. For example, we may be tempted to be angry, but something tells us to control our troubles and frustrations. Flying carelessly off the handle at someone else solves nothing. It can only deepen the problem.

However, we must learn to say, "I don't want to be natural. I want to be supernatural." You can say, "I don't want to act like what some people may classify as 'normal', because when I do, I can be difficult. I want to be 'mature'. I don't want to be me. I want to be what I was created to be!"

Someone has said, "We need to find ourselves." Well, I found myself and I did not like what I found! Therefore, I realized that I needed to be conformed into what I was meant to be. One of the greatest blessings I can receive is controlling my emotions, thoughts, and actions to be a blessing to others.

Identifying our personalities can help us become wiser, but first, we need to understand more about our personalities. While most educational institutions do not specifically address the science of human behavior and personality types, we certainly can learn a lot about it from those who have researched and developed the theories over the past 2400 years.

Overview of the 4 DISC Model of Human Behavior.

The terms "personality" and "temperament" are synonymous to most people. When we use these terms, we are referring to patterns of thoughts, feelings, and behaviors. There are many theories about personality types. After much study, I chose to use the DISC Model because it is simple to understand, easy to remember, and practical to apply.

Understanding our active or passive roles (extroverts and introverts) helps us identify our specific temperament styles. By combining these two different categories of influences, along with our task and people-orientations, we end up with four specific types.

Everyone has a predictable pattern of behavior because of his or her specific personality. There are four basic personality types. These types, also known as temperaments, blend together to determine your unique personality. To help you understand why you often feel, think, and act the way you do, the following graphic summarizes the *Four Temperament Model of Human Behavior:*

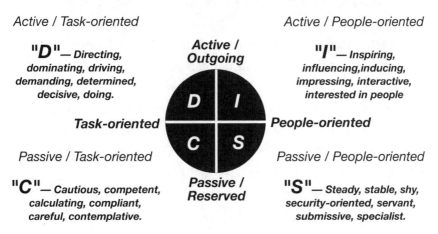

Active / Task-oriented

"D"— *Directing, dominating, driving, demanding, determined, decisive, doing.*

Active / Outgoing

Active / People-oriented

"I"— *Inspiring, influencing,inducing, impressing, interactive, interested in people*

Task-oriented

D | I

C | S

People-oriented

Passive / Task-oriented

"C"— *Cautious, competent, calculating, compliant, careful, contemplative.*

Passive / Reserved

Passive / People-oriented

"S"— *Steady, stable, shy, security-oriented, servant, submissive, specialist.*

Some people are easily identifiable as active extroverts or passive introverts, but many of us are confused because not all extroverts are active toward people. Some are active in tasks. In the same way, introverts can be passive in relation to people or tasks. Understanding the four quadrant model of basic human behavior sheds light on this. It can make the difference between the right and wrong response, and a proper or improper behavior in any given situation.

Historical Background Of Personality Types

The *Four Temperament Model of Human Behavior* is attributed to Hippocrates, the father of modern medicine. His scientific research and brilliant observations are nearly universally accepted. Contrary to what critics claim, the Four Temperaments did not hatch from archaic pagan Greek philosophy, but rather the scientific process that made Hippocrates the most respected physician in his day.

The DISC Model of Human Behavior was first introduced by William Marston in 1928 through his book, *The Emotions Of Normal People.* Marston took Hippocrates' Greek titles and assigned simple and single D, I, S, and C letters to each type. Though there are now many titles to various models, they all have roots from the same basic four temperaments discovered around 400 B.C.

Dr. John Geier, Chairman of the Human Behavior Science Department at the University of Minnesota, designed the first paper assessment that identified a person's DISC personality type from a business and personal perspective in 1977.

After studying under Dr. Geier with Performax Systems and Dr. Frank Wichern, Staff Psychologist at Dallas Theological

Seminary, I designed the first-of-its-kind combination personality and faith-based gifts profiles. With over one million of my profiles now in print in several different languages, my *Uniquely You profiles* are some of the most respected and popular profiles available for businesses, personal use, and faith-based organizations.

Understanding the four-quadrant model of basic human behavior often explains why people do what they do. These insights can make the difference between right and wrong responses, and the best or worst behavior in most situations.

To receive maximum effectiveness, be sure to complete your personality profile by going online at: *www.uniquelyyou.NET*, then click on "For Professionals / Leaders." There are so many insights for you to learn! See page 8 for more instructions.

There are also Behavioral Blends that are specific to you. The profile is not a psychological analysis. It is not designed to deal with serious emotional problems. It *can* help with simple insights into basic human behavior motivations. For more in-depth needs, we recommend you seek professional counseling.

Hippocrates observed four unique temperament types, or four specific patterns of behavior. He thought it had something to do with the chemical makeup of the blood. To describe the four types, he used Greek words which have been Anglicized as: choleric, sanguine, phlegmatic, and melancholy. Many researchers who observe human behavior have categorized people into four temperaments, but most scientists have concluded that personalities have nothing to do with the color of body fluids!

People tend to think that ancient science is out-of-date and irrelevant. True science is not irrelevant. It does not matter how old the truth is. What is true today will be true tomorrow. Understanding personalities is an ancient science with modern implications and practical applications.

You can correlate the Greek terms to the DISC model:

- "D" is the Choleric.
- "I" is the Sanguine.
- "S" is the Phlegmatic.
- "C" is the Melancholy.

A Quick Look

Our personalities should never become an excuse for poor behavior. The attitude of many is: "That's just the way I am. Love me or leave me. You knew I was like that when you married me," but we should not blame our rotten reactions on our personalities.

Each temperament style represents a specific behavior pattern. How we use or abuse our personalities determines our effectiveness with others. Once we understand the four quadrant model of behavior styles, we can begin to identify our individual profile. To simplify the four types of temperaments, we will use William Marston's *DISC titles*. The following are the four quadrants of the DISC model:

- "D" — active / task-oriented
- "I" — active / people-oriented
- "S" — passive / people-oriented
- "C" — passive / task-oriented

Once you burn the four quadrants in your mind you can begin to easily identify the different personality types. It will also help you become more effective in your work and home.

NASA's Head of Mission Control

While I was conducting training in Houston near NASA, a gentleman came up to me after the seminar and asked if I would autograph a copy of my book, *What Makes You Tick and What Ticks You Off.* The person behind him asked me if I knew who this man was. I realized he must be someone important.

He then introduced me to the Head of Mission Control at NASA. The man said I had fascinated him with my illustration of how rocket scientists could communicate with satellites millions of miles away in outer space, but found it difficult to know how to communicate effectively with coworkers who were just a few feet away. When we think of this example it is easy to see how people can be "computer-smart" but so "people-dumb." I also want to add the fact that we can be philosophically and theologically "smart," while being "people-dumb" and / or insensitive to the needs and emotions of others.

The sad truth is that the more we develop and improve our machines, computers, and technology - which have no emotions — the less effective we are to those around us — our loved ones, our friends, and our coworkers. This is why we should learn and practice better people skills. We must not allow technology to become a substitute for our abilities to feel and care for others. I cannot overemphasize the importance of nurturing and improving all our relationships with others.

People can be a combination of active and passive, while task- or people-oriented.

There are many composites and blends of behaviors. Our personalities lean toward certain directions that guide our behavior

23

in different situations.

Understanding our active/passive roles helps identify our specific temperament style. Identifying these four different types can be very enlightening. As we will see, some people are a mixture of both active and passive, while being both task- and people-oriented at the same time.

Most people know if they are active extroverts or passive introverts. However, there can be confusion and frustration because not all extroverts are active toward people — some are active toward task accomplishments. In the same way, introverts can be passive in relation to people and / or tasks.

There are definite differences between task- and people-oriented behavior. To illustrate this, let us say a "task" type person and a "people" person are both working in a garden. Someone walks up and says, "Hi, how are you — what's happening?" How will the task-person predictably respond? Obviously, he or she will say something like, "I'm busy," or "Come back later." The task-person tends to be so concerned about getting the job done that he or she does not care about socializing.

How will the people-person predictably respond? "Good to see you. It's a great time for a break. Let's talk." The people-person does not care nearly as much about getting the garden done as he or she does about developing relationships.

Understanding the four-quadrant model of basic human behavior sheds light on why this is so. It can make the difference between right and wrong responses, and help us discern the best or worst behavior in any situation.

DISC Descriptions

Following is a simple description of each of the four types of behavior represented by the letters D-I-S-C. A strong or high type behavior is more obvious and predictable than a weak or low type.

"D" Behavior—

"D"s are determined leaders. They can take control of a situation, make quick decisions, and cause things to happen. If they overuse their strengths, they can become dictatorial, demanding, or domineering.

"I" Behavior—

High "I"s are optimistic people who lead by inspiring, influencing, and inducing others to follow. They may be characterized by overconfidence, talkativeness, and a craving for popularity. These individuals tend to compromise their beliefs due to peer pressure.

"S" Behavior—

High "S"s are stable, submissive, and steady. They do not like change and are extremely loyal. The most tolerant of all, these people are often timid and too agreeable.

"C" Behavior—

Strong "C"s are cautious, calculating, and conservative. They are seldom wrong because they are slow to decide. However, these individuals tend to overanalyze and be too critical of others.

Strengths and Weaknesses

Each personality has its strengths and weaknesses. Conflict or harmony in relationships is the result of how we use or abuse our personalities in response to life's situations.

Keep in mind that 85% of people tend to be composites of DISC; therefore, most people will be blends and combinations of the characteristics evident in the four personalities. There are numerous variations of this model. Speakers, writers, and trainers have added their own titles to make the model more simple or personal, but this four vector explanation of basic human behavior has become very popular. *The DISC personality profile* (paper instrument) was originally designed by Dr. John Geier and has been validated by the Kaplan Report and Winchester Report. The DISC profile and Model of Human Behavior stands out as one of the most reliable and practical available today.

Basic Overview of the DISC Model

Psychologist Dr. Frank Wichern introduced me to a full description of the four temperament types while I attended Dallas Theological Seminary. I want to include his insights here, which I have modified in a few places. You may want to add characteristics to this list as you learn more about people's patterns of behavior.

High "D"s

BASIC MOTIVATION:
- Challenge

ENVIRONMENTAL NEEDS:
- Freedom
- Authority
- Varied activities
- Difficult assignments
- Opportunity for advancement

RESPONDS BEST TO A LEADER WHO:
- Provides direct answers
- Sticks to business
- Stresses goals
- Provides pressure
- Allows freedom for personal accomplishment

NEEDS TO LEARN THAT:
- People are important
- Relaxation is not a crime
- Some controls are needed
- Everyone has a boss
- Verbalizing conclusions helps other people understand them better

High "I"s

BASIC MOTIVATION:
- Recognition

ENVIRONMENTAL NEEDS:
- Prestige
- Friendly relationships
- Opportunities to influence others
- Opportunities to inspire people
- Chance to verbalize ideas

RESPONDS BEST TO A LEADER WHO:
- Is a democratic manager and a friend
- Provides social involvement outside of work
- Provides recognition of abilities
- Offers incentives for risk-taking

NEEDS TO LEARN THAT:
- Time must be managed
- There is such a thing as too much optimism
- Details are important
- Humility is a virtue

High "S"s

BASIC MOTIVATION:
- Security

ENVIRONMENTAL NEEDS:
- An area of specialization
- Identification with a group
- Established work pattern
- Stability of situation
- Consistent, familiar environment

RESPONDS BEST TO A LEADER WHO:
- Is relaxed and amiable
- Allows time to adjust to change in plans
- Serves as a friend
- Allows people to work at their own pace
- Answers "how" questions
- Clearly defines goals and means of reaching them
- Gives personal support

NEEDS TO LEARN THAT:
- Change provides opportunity
- Friendship isn't everything
- Discipline is good

High "C"s

BASIC MOTIVATION:
- Quality

ENVIRONMENTAL NEEDS:
- Clearly defined tasks
- Sufficient time and resources to accomplish tasks
- Explanations
- Team participation
- Limited risks
- Assignments that require precision and planning

RESPONDS BEST TO A LEADER WHO:
- Provides reassurance
- Maintains a supportive atmosphere
- Provides open door policy
- Defines concise, detailed operating standards

NEEDS TO LEARN THAT:
- Total support is not always necessary
- Thorough explanation is not always possible
- Deadlines must be met

Once you get a good picture of the DISC Model of Human Behavior, you should then see the value of profiling people. The thought of profiling may be offensive or have a bad connotation, but there is a place for legitimately profiling people. We profile blood types to help save lives. We also profile criminals to solve crimes. Profiling can be used for many good purposes.

Point #2

Understanding DISC personality types often explains why people do what they do!

People respond to discovering their personality types in many different ways. Some people find it fascinating, while others find it frustrating. For some, identifying their temperaments is easy. For others, it can be extremely difficult. Some people are more obviously one or two personality types, while others are a unique blend. If your personality fits into one or two categories, it is easier to identify and understand your specific personality.

Most people quickly recognize their strengths and uniqueness, but some feel they are a composite of every type. This may cause confusion. Evaluation is not always easy, so be honest with yourself and focus on those characteristics which are obvious. Disregard the descriptions which do not fit. Narrow it down to one or two types which best describe you.

Your personality may even shape your response to this study. "D"s are sometimes proud of their type. "I"s tend to be more excited and talkative about their personality. "S"s are more shy and quiet. "C"s are usually the most inquisitive.

I often have people come to me after a seminar and say, "Is this really valid? I don't know if I agree with my profile."

I respond, "I can prove how valid it is. You're a High "C", aren't you?"

They invariably look surprised and ask, "How did you know?"

And I explain, "C's always ask the same questions. They doubt the validity and need more explanation."

Some people are afraid to identify their personalities. I try to reassure them that their assessment is not a test and there are no wrong answers. They can not fail it. It simply profiles their personality types, and no one has a bad personality. A few people have had bad experiences with psychological testing, and they feel hesitant to try another tool.

The *Uniquely You Personality Profile*, however, is not a clinical measurement. It is designed for people who simply want to understand a little more about themselves and others. People who struggle most over personality profiling are often pessimistic about themselves. They sometimes suffer from a poor self-image. They have trouble seeing their personalities as unique gifts, and they are afraid of change and control.

We have just taken a brief overview of the DISC types. Now let us take a closer look at each type as it stands alone. Keep in mind that most people have a blend or combination of "D," "I," "S," and "C" behavior. We will identify the different Behavioral Blends later. Look at each personality type to see how each one responds independent of the others.

Controlling The Dominant Personality

When you think of the people who seem to be natural leaders, who accept challenges, who are involved in many different projects, and who are more task- than people-oriented, you are thinking of high "D"s.

"D"s are:
- Dominant
- Direct
- Determined
- Demanding
- Doers

"D"s push for results. They shape the environment by overcoming opposition. They are very active, and they create aggressive environments, striving and pushing under pressure to get the job done. Also known as the "Rocky Cholerics," they are the rough, tough Rambo types. They love action-oriented challenges. "D"s tend to cause action or trouble, depending on how they respond to stress. They constantly question the status quo. Their motto is, "If it doesn't work, change it." They take charge; they want to be in control. They were most likely the self-appointed captains of teams (or even leaders of gangs) growing up.

"D"s are often raised to dominate and direct the action of others. Our fathers and mothers are the greatest influences in shaping behavior. Parents who possess strong leadership qualities and determined personalities tend to produce high "D" children.

"D"s want control and authority. They often believe they know how to do things better than anyone else and instinctively take charge, but they also work well under authority if they respect their superiors and remember who is the boss.

These determined people need challenge and prestige to fulfill their dreams. They seek opportunities for individual accomplishments and work their way to the top. They become CEOs, owners of their own businesses, or top managers in any field, club, or organization. Even if they do not climb the corporate ladder, "D"s end up telling everyone what to do. They can be found ordering others how to dig a ditch or organizing a local union.

Dictators or Doormats?

"D"s are definitely not doormats. They do not like anyone to step on them. They tend to be dictatorial, and they would be more effective if they developed skills of delegation. They have the ability to dream, but they usually are not strong in following through with the details. Therefore, these visionaries need to be able to delegate what they feel is mundane or time consuming.

For "D"s, stumbling blocks are stepping stones. Nothing is too difficult. They want freedom from controls and supervision, so they often become their own bosses. They move fast and hard and are the most prone to become workaholics. Confronted with conflicts, they are quick problem-solvers, but they seldom calculate all the risks or consider all the options.

"D"s are instinctively impatient. They do not put off until tomorrow what they can do today. They push forward despite time limitations. Often misunderstood because of their active, task-oriented, optimistic personalities, these driven individuals are often tough-skinned and hard-nosed. They act as if the world is going to end tomorrow, therefore the project or plan must be finished today! Their emotions can be extremely intense.

Superman and Superwoman

"D"s sometimes seem to accomplish the impossible. They are not quitters. These driven people love a challenge and are very competitive. They have a "do or die" attitude toward life. As active extroverts, they like to be where the action is. They are unable to stand still for long periods of time. Most of all, they love to direct the action of others. As task-oriented individuals, "D"s absorb themselves in projects rather than people. Often they seem to intimidate people to accomplish their jobs. They use people to build their work rather than use their work to build people. It is not that they do not care about people. They are just more concerned about the projects. People are a means to the end of getting the job done. "D"s appear cold and hard, but life's pruning process can cause them to be more tolerant and caring. Experience and maturity teach them to be more people-oriented.

Dominant types are impatient and easily irritated by those who are indecisive. They like strong leadership. They are purpose-driven. They love challenges, so conflict is normal for them. They seem to relish debate and defiance. Tell "D"s they can not do something, and a startling metamorphosis begins to take place. They can turn into monsters! They attack!

They need to be more calm and understanding of others' feelings. "D"s are often too straightforward and frank. They need to think before reacting. To improve their effectiveness in relationships, these people must control themselves rather than trying to control others.

Two "D"s working together will struggle for control. Ultimately, one will dominate while the other reluctantly submits to survive. Two dominant people jockey for position until someone wins the coveted place of being on top.

This can lead toward bitterness. The only difference in the words "bitter" and "better" is the letter "i." Each of us must answer for our actions, thoughts, and feelings.

After all is said from both sides of a conflict, only you can decide to do right. You can not force others to accept your humble apology for how you have disappointed them. You can not make them admit their wrongs. As a "D", you should not try to control everyone. In any conflict, you should love and respect others in spite of their faults.

Who's The Boss?

A high "D" will try to control someone with a low "D" score and make all the decisions. The other often sheepishly obeys. Low "D"s willingly follow along in submission until their most serious concerns are challenged.

Low "D" people find it very difficult to confront high "D"s. Their best preparation for battle is accurate information to prove their point. Presenting high "D"s with analysis usually causes them to look more closely at the conflict and be more rational.

As bosses, "D"s are usually domineering and demand a lot of their employees. They are strong leaders. They lean toward absolutes; everything is "right or wrong," and compromise is uncomfortable.

In marriage, two dominant people need to learn to communicate clearly and respect each other's goals and desires. I recently met two "D"s who had been married for some time. They were both strong-willed and aggressive. Their marriage had become void of feelings. Little communication existed, but they seemed fairly happy. I honestly wondered, "How can they be happy?" They explained they never made a major decision unless they both agreed. It seemed to work, and I was impressed.

It is uncommon for the marriage of two "D"s to survive through child raising, buying homes, and growing old because they often feel pressured by the other. The trials and troubles of life often prove too great a strain on the relationship because they both have to win. But two "D"s *can* have great marriages, when they both learn to love each other unconditionally.

Under pressure, our strengths become our weaknesses. We are more comfortable and confident in the roles, qualities, and abilities we know best. A "D" tends to become more dominant and demanding under pressure. When the going gets tough, the "D"s get going . . . right for the jugular! They tend to steam roll and subdue their opposition, and force of character is often their style of confronting. "Do something! Lead, follow, or get out of the way!" is their approach to dealing with stress. Their leadership ability is an attribute, but carried to an extreme, it becomes dictatorial.

In many situations, someone needs to take charge. All Indians and no Chief usually means mass chaos and confusion, and "D"s are glad to be the Chiefs. They are decisive leaders, and in emergencies their powers of thinking and decision-making are heightened. They go from zero to hero or hero to zero, depending on how they handle the challenge.

Doers, Not Thinkers

"D"s' greatest influence over others is their ability to accomplish goals. Though careless at times, they usually still produce results. They tend to make people nervous because they are producers, pushers, and movers. They make great achievers if they do not self-destruct. They often speak before thinking, but surprisingly, they often come up with unique and immediate solutions. These results give them the confidence to "fly by the seat of their pants."

Other people, however, do not feel comfortable with this free-wheeling style, so "D"s need to be more considerate of others. Dominant, demanding people tend to overlook little things that make others feel apprehensive. Absorbed in task-oriented projects, they cause high casualty rates among subordinates and co-workers. Their "herd mentality" of getting everyone moving in the same direction at the same time is demeaning to others who prefer to be treated as individuals.

"D"s are sometimes great motivators and challenging speakers, but their greatest concern is "reaching the mark, not touching the heart." By learning to balance their penchant for tasks with concern for people, "D"s can be much more effective leaders.

Though "D"s occasionally delegate work, they usually feel compelled to do everything themselves to maintain control and have it done "the right way." Once they learn to spread the responsibility around, they should supervise—but not smother—those who are contributing to the task.

One of their biggest faults is taking back delegated responsibility. To "save" a project, they may take back control and offend the one who was placed in charge. "D"s need to learn to communicate the purpose, plan, and process more effectively with others. Unfortunately, they believe the myth that everyone else thinks and feels as they do.

"D"s prefer techniques based on practical experience. Though they are pragmatic, they tend to theorize too much. More detailed approaches would improve their results.

Remembering their ethics and values is imperative. They tend to lose sight of truth while focusing on the finish line. Winning at the expense of character is a defeat with a crown. Success apart from the proper means is a loss.

"D"s are tireless workers wherever they go, but they can become too task-oriented, too demanding, and too decisive. They need to remember that only a few people are like them. Most people are more sensitive and thoughtful. Typically insensitive, demanding people can markedly increase their effectiveness by being more people-oriented. "D"s are change agents, but most people do not want change. "D" leaders are often misunderstood. Their dreams and drives scare people, but when they earn respect and trust, they can lead the organization to great heights.

An occasional shock brings confident, dominant individuals back to earth. Experience is their best teacher, and their overconfidence is tempered by the painful consequences of bad decisions from time to time. To be most successful, they need difficult assignments. They are easily bored and need constant challenge, but they need to stay focused on the most important task and see it through to the end.

"D" behavior enjoys challenging crowds but should focus on the individual's needs. The results will be evident as "D"s learn the principle of "being as big as all but as small as one."

Slow Down and Explain

Once a decision is made on how a task should be accomplished, "D"s should tell others the reasons behind their decisions. Though they may be convinced and confident of that decision, others may not be. Clear and patient explanations enhance a person's role in leadership. It is not enough to simply say, "Because!" or "I'm the boss!" Reasons and specific plans need to be verbalized for everyone to feel secure in the decision.

"D"s are often like the Pony Express: Nothing can stop them! They need to pace themselves and learn to relax. Vacations can provide the needed balance for their high stress levels. Physical conditioning is vital because stress is one of their worst enemies! They are often unaware of the tremendous pressure they put on themselves to produce, and they are prime candidates for heart attacks and hypertension. Learning to relax and enjoy life should be part of their plans to succeed. Vance Havner said, "If we don't learn to come apart for a while and rest, we may just come apart!"

Most importantly, these driven people need to learn to prioritize. Working overtime and seldom pausing to appreciate their mates and children are hazardous to their health and wealth. The twin tyrannies of urgency and expedience are dilemmas they must avoid.

As weekend mechanics with finely tuned machines, "D"s seem to race through life without the worries of blowouts. They are most effective when they slow down, calculate the risks, weigh the options, and receive wise counsel from others. Reflection and balance will protect them from their volatile emotions which can ignite their dynamite personalities.

The best way to relate to "D"s is in a straightforward manner. Do not beat around the bush. Get to the bottom line. They will certainly get to the bottom line with you! I once encouraged a fund raiser salesman who was going to meet with a high "D" school administrator to not waste his time.

The salesperson was a high "I," and sometimes he talked too much. I advised him to get right to the point in his meeting. He told me later that he walked into the administrator's office and said, "Mels told me you're a high 'D', so here's what I can do for you."

He took thirty minutes and walked out with a $40,000 sale.

"D"s need choices. Parents and teachers of high "D" children need to harness their energy. Relate to them by showing respect for their ability to decide for themselves. Give them opportunities to be leaders. Do not stifle their drives. Point them in the right direction, give them parameters, and watch them fly!

These driven people are the best doers anywhere. They conquer life's greatest challenges, but unfortunately they seldom conquer themselves. When you think of steel and velvet, dominant people are characterized by steel, but they need to be sensitive to others. "D"s are drivers plowing their way through life, but they need to pave their way with pleasantness.

Calming The Inspiring Personality Type

I once underestimated the power of charisma, and in the process I strained a good relationship. In the mid '80s, a leader in our church wanted to start a coffee house ministry. "Hootenannies" and coffee houses were no longer effective ministry vehicles for reaching young people, but my leader friend still thought it was a good idea.

He was an effective communicator. He and his wife were very popular in the church. She had a beautiful voice. He could also sing, and his gift was grass roots evangelism and discipleship. Our church was outreach-oriented, so he thought the coffee house idea would be a winner. When he brought it to the leader's meeting, I expressed my concerns because I felt he had a problem with pride. He wanted to be center stage at every church event, including our worship services.

I decided to talk to him about his pride, and to my amazement, he confessed his fault in one of our more heated leader's meetings. He placed himself on a temporary leave of absence. Later, when I learned more about personality types, I felt very guilty for the way I had treated him. I did not understand the nature of his powerful personality, and I should have appreciated his abilities more. I should have encouraged him with his idea, or at least helped him shape it. But instead, I fought it.

I now realize that some people are born to shine. (Sometimes they shine even more than I do!) My responsibility is not to throw a blanket over their light. I need to help make their talents brighter! My ministry has been greatly blessed by understanding how certain people stand out above the rest.

Perhaps the easiest temperament to identify is the "I." They are the "Sparky Sanguines" of life. You will find them leading, entertaining, and somehow adding to the positive atmosphere of every occasion.

"I"s are:
- Inspiring
- Influencing
- Interested in people
- Impressive
- Inducing

Naturally uninhibited, "I"s love to express themselves. They are the clowns of the class and the life of the party. Often raised in a family atmosphere that encouraged them to share their talents openly, "I"s are performers and people-pleasers. Their charisma and abilities to sway the crowd make them naturally persuasive speakers, salespersons, or actors.

"I"s who work in sales positions sometimes have difficulty closing deals because they do not want to be rejected. A "no" is a blow to their pride. Although "I"s give the impression of high ego strength like "D"s, they are much more sensitive to being hurt and manipulated than their domineering counterparts. Their charisma and ability to communicate only gives the illusion of inner strength.

Inspiring, sensitive people in sales may be more concerned about making a good impression than selling the product. I once helped a furniture store owner interview a prospective salesperson. The lady was a high "I" with great selling ability. I wanted to teach her how strengths can become weaknesses, and how her communication skills could become her downfall. I said, "Let me prove something to you," then paused. There was a moment of silence.

She broke the silence with, "What are you trying to prove?"

And I said, "I just proved it." Then I paused again, even longer.

The silence was deafening, so she said anxiously, "I don't understand. What did you just prove?"

I said, "I just proved it again," then paused once more.

Obviously confused, she rattled, "This is scary! What did you just prove?"

I finally explained, "Every time I paused, you had to speak. You couldn't stand the silence. Good salespeople know when to talk and when to ask questions. The best salespeople are those who get customers to talk themselves into buying the product."

Happy Faces

"I"s want to bring others together to get results. They are active individuals who create positive environments for others. They are optimists, and they work best through people. One of their greatest strengths is the ability to relate to people; they are easily accepted and popular. They communicate well with others because they can use words and emotions effectively.

In 1984, Dr. Tim LaHaye arranged for me to be invited to a special briefing with President Ronald Reagan in the White House. The briefing focused on the American family and traditional values. I remember being in a elevator crowded with a group of preachers on board. The door closed and no one said a word. The seconds seemed like an eternity. Everyone wanted to say something, but we all waited for someone else to break the silence. Finally, one of the pastors said, "This is a great crowd for an offering." We all laughed and I thought to myself, "He's definitely an 'I.'"

"I"s are the people who make small talk in the checkout lines at supermarkets. While other shoppers look for the shortest or fastest lane, "I"s enjoy the opportunity to socialize with people. They like to help other shoppers in the store whether they work there or not. If someone looks confused, "I"s naturally respond, "Can I help you?" They enjoy making people feel good.

Cheerleaders At Heart

"I"s are cheerleaders. Even when they are not up front, they stimulate those around them. They are natural spark plugs. They generate tremendous enthusiasm, and they entertain people. "I"s want to help others to feel good or accomplish a goal. They love to participate in groups where they can stand out. "I"s often take control of a group, not because of a strong desire to have their say, but because others will not. In order to avoid feeling uncomfortable, they naturally step out and lead.

These influencers prefer environments which include acceptance and social recognition. They are very friendly and enjoy back slapping, hugging, and encouraging others. They fill the air with laughter and joy.

Recognition is a strong incentive for "I"s. They desire the freedom of individual expression to win approval. Their unique ability to speak spontaneously about anything and everything often gains them recognition in crowds. They can be found in an abundance of group activities outside their jobs. Where there is a crowd, there is an "I." Relaxing alone is not their style; they need and seek relationships. Because of their friendly demeanor, their interests are often crowd-centered.

A recent experiment proved how persuasive "I"s can be. Several preschoolers were asked to lie about the taste of some juice during snack time. They were told that the teacher's friend made the juice and needed to be told how good it was. The juice tasted terrible.

After sampling the juice all the children agreed it tasted terrible, but they promised to say it tasted good. When the teacher's friend met each of the students individually, certain children could not hide the fact that they did not like it. They said the juice was good, but their body language and nonverbal communication said they were lying.

Other students, however, hid their feelings. They enthusiastically shared how much they liked the juice. Their open, bubbly, high "I" personalities covered up the truth. They were able to lie convincingly about an unquestionable fact. Interestingly, the students who could lie without showing it were the ones who were leaders during playtime. The students who could not hide their feelings became followers. Those who lied were more active and aggressive, and they spent most of playtime telling the passive, honest kids what to do.

I am obviously not advocating lying, but I am warning "I" personalities to be careful with reality. They must guard their persuasive personalities and always speak the truth.

Work Environment

"I"s will never be slaves to time. They do not like time controls because they have trouble pulling themselves away from people. The task at hand is never as important as the people with whom they want to talk. Details are often seen as stumbling blocks. With broad, sweeping, verbal strokes, "I"s can easily fly right over the nitty gritty, leaving details to others. They are concerned about new opportunities for recognition and acceptance, so opportunities to verbalize their proposals or ideas are very important to them.

Their strong need for favorable working conditions frustrates them when they are confronted with adversity. High "I"s need to concentrate on the task at hand. They are easily distracted, especially if they are working alone. "I"s are often tempted to help someone or just stop and talk rather than work productively alone. They need others who respect their sincerity. They tend to give confusing messages about themselves, and they are often misunderstood as being proud or cocky. In reality, they are very sensitive to what people think.

"I"s need to focus on the facts because many of their decisions are based on emotions. They need to learn to collect more information and consider all the options before coming to a conclusion.

They tend to jump into things and they make great initiators. Because they desire to talk so much, they often say whatever comes off the tops of their heads, and this may make them sound ambiguous and shallow. They should concentrate more on getting to the point and being specific.

Being surrounded by others who have systematic approaches to problem-solving is very beneficial to these inspiring people. They need others who can deal with details and design the systems of follow-through to accomplish tasks. "I"s make "great ideas" employees. They can be extremely creative, but they need to focus on getting the job done. I can tell you that I have started a million jobs and finished only a few. People say I am creative, but I often wonder what they say about all my unfinished "great ideas." In the first half of my life, I concentrated on starting lots of new, innovative projects. But now in the last half of my life, I am working harder on finishing well.

Strong Feelings

Because "I"s are primarily guided by feelings, they need to focus on the process of decision-making and individual follow-through. They are easily distracted and tend to be undisciplined and disorganized. Training themselves to sit and think on their own is an important step in their work habits. Instead of constantly seeking an ear to listen to them, they need to do more research in order to become more self-efficient.

"I"s need to practice taking a logical (rather than a social) approach to their problem-solving. They need to learn to demonstrate individual stick-to-it-ness. As promoters and persuaders, "I"s have the ability to spark interest and enthusiasm in others for just about anything. If, however, they lack the drive to see tasks through to completion, their energy and power of persuasion are wasted. They should constantly strive to perfect their follow-through and complete what they have started. Organizational skills to help them manage their tasks include clock watching, scheduling, and personal planning.

Some "I" children are misunderstood by their parents. These excitable, enthusiastic kids may be tagged "hyperactive," but in reality, they are only being themselves. Parents of "I" children need to give a lot of positive strokes because these kids need more approval and recognition than others. (Keep in mind, all children respond best to affirming, optimistic influences.) Pessimistic parents can be very discouraging to these sensitive children. Interactive parents make great encouragers, but poor examples. "I"s tend to be too dramatic, and as parents, they can be "screamers." Their overly expressive behavior makes "I" children reactive. "I" parents need to learn to control their emotions and be calm. Children learn how to react by watching their parents, so screaming parents usually produce screaming kids.

"I"s need to control their time more wisely. They are often defeated by the clock, overwhelmed by the pressure of schedules and deadlines because they naturally mismanage their time. They should realize that there is not time for everyone and everything in the day.

Think before doing

Thinking ahead and planning for interruptions are practical steps. Because "I" types talk so much, they usually take a lot of time to complete tasks, so they should give themselves more leeway in terms of when they might realistically complete a task. It is wise for them to set time limits and schedule earlier deadlines. Talking does not always solve problems and accomplish tasks. In fact, conversation often prolongs a project. In order to be productive, "I"s must learn the value of solitude and silence.

Those who plan time alone can better manage their natural ability to interact with others. Also, they should respect the time restrictions of other people's schedules. Silence is an important commodity for these gregarious people to acquire. They will become more objective if they think before expressing themselves. They should consider the amount of time and thought they have given a matter before coming to any conclusions. "I"s should weigh their words wisely before speaking.

Although they tend to get away with things because they are popular, they should strive to be "slow to speak and quick to listen." They can avoid "me-first-itis" by going out of their way to include people in discussions and decision-making. Learning to let others speak for themselves is essential, and allowing others to share in the "limelight" forces "I"s to take a back seat.

Because of their confidence and uninhibited personalities, "I"s tend to think more highly of themselves than of others. A more realistic appraisal of their associates can be humbling. Letting others go first and sharing the spotlight minimizes the possibility that "I"s will be criticized for pride.

Competing Partners

"I" spouses tend to be too communicative, and they can be too sensitive about feelings. "I"s often want to know what their mates are thinking, but they seldom wait for answers. When a person tries to express themself, "I"s interrupt and never let the person finish. "I"s need to be patient and focus on the other person. They also need to be careful not to concentrate on what they are going to say as soon as the person pauses to take a breath.

I know of a couple who have enough "I" in them that their conversations tend to get exciting. They are both very expressive! A friend dropped in on them while they were in the middle of one of their verbal battles. Since they are all good friends, the couple decided to share with their friend who dropped by, the husband's frustrations about his wife's picky perfectionism. She interrupted and clarified every other sentence. He also interrupted and heard little of what she said.

He overreacted and got angry! She eventually left the room crying. Their poor friend never expected this! It is one of the few times in many years of marriage that they ever had a spat in public, but the husband learned a tremendous lesson. Their friend observed that neither of them listened to the other because they were so intent on talking. They will never forget the timely advice.

Once you have shared your feelings, ask the person listening to repeat what he or she heard. What the husband says is often not what the wife hears, and vice versa. We are all responsible for making what we say clear. It is never the wife's fault for not hearing the husband correctly. Since the day their friend showed them how to communicate better, the husband has often said, "I'm so sorry I didn't make myself clear. Let me try again."

This perspective works a lot better than accusing the other of not listening! Do not criticize your mate for not hearing what you are saying. I often say in training seminars, "The teacher hasn't taught until the students have learned."

"I" partners compete for the air waves, and they can also compete for attention. Two "I"s in a marriage or working relationship can become jealous of each other. They must learn to appreciate one another's talents and be willing to learn from each other rather than constantly telling the other what to do.

They sincerely want to express themselves, but they need to remember that the other person may have the same desire. A little understanding and a lot of patience can go a long way with two "I"s. They demonstrate maturity and love when they allow someone else to have center stage.

Because "I"s are sensitive, they tend to avoid offending people. They need to learn that being firm and honest can be more important to others than being friendly. They have a keen sense of the mood of groups of people. This makes them natural leaders with the ability to inspire and influence people. Their friendliness is a blessing at every function.

Sources of Conflict

"I"s over-promise and under-deliver. Desiring to please everyone, they build high expectations, and people are often disappointed by their unfulfilled promises. When asked to do something, it is better to respond, "I'd rather let you know than to let you down. Let me get back to you about whether I can do what you ask."

They also struggle when they do not get the credit or attention they deserve. If they feel overlooked, they can be very expressive about their disappointment.

They may irritate others by talking too much, not being on time, and being disorganized. Conflicts often arise with those who are more task-oriented, but "I"s usually relate well to people-oriented people. They make great first impressions but must work to avoid conflicts because of irresponsibility and the appearance of laziness. Also, they need to control their feelings and make decisions based on reason.

Emotionally, "I"s tend to experience extreme highs and lows. The "downs" typically do not last long however, and they quickly return to their optimism. They also tend to wear their feelings on their sleeves. They may discover that it is beneficial at times to keep their feelings to themselves and wait for the right time to express them. Their enthusiastic and exciting personalities make others glad to know them. Life would be boring without "I"s!

Relating To Relational Types

These influential people are extremely relational, but sometimes they are too "touchy feely." They respond best to those who allow them to express their feelings. They need genuine compliments; do not flatter them. Recognize their beauty and talents, and try to reinforce positive character traits as well as their accomplishments. Allow them to shine and share. Do not stifle their creativity or pull the plug on their energy, but encourage them to use their abilities. They need to guard against their desire for honor and recognition.. "I"s can become persuasive leaders, but they need to remember to make others look better than they look.

Stimulating The Shy Personality

The highest percentage of people fall into the category of the passive, people-oriented type of personality. They are shy and reserved, but they often make the best friends and most loyal employees.

Perhaps you have heard of individuals who took the blame for things they did not do. They willingly accepted punishment, even though they were not guilty. History has given us many lessons of those who suffered for the short-comings of others. Loyalty motivates some people to suffer for the wrongs of others. They would rather endure pain themselves than to allow others to hurt. This can be a wonderful quality, but it can also be a dangerous fault.

I have seen my wife, who is so loving and sacrificing, give of herself rather than let anyone down. She is always willing to help others, regardless of how she might feel. Her personality is sweet and sensitive, and everyone loves her. She has a "S" type personality.

"S"s are:
- Stable
- Steady
- Security-oriented
- Sensitive

"S"s emphasize cooperating with others to carry out tasks. They are submissive servants who usually end up doing what the "D" has dreamed and the "I" has promoted. "S"s are soft-hearted and sensitive. They may be seen as timid, but they are tireless in their labor. They let others lead, they avoid conflicts, and they strive for the status quo. Change is difficult for them, so innovation and creativity are left to others.

These people prefer sitting or staying in a single place. Their passiveness is often perceived as laziness by extroverts, but they are steady work horses. They quietly get the job done while others push, talk, play, or criticize. "S"s do not like to make waves. Instead, they work to calm others, creating stability and security around them. Tranquility in the midst of turmoil is their specialty. Their staying power is incredible. While others lose their patience, nothing seems to unravel these steady, reliable people. They seldom openly show their feelings, and if they do, they quietly cry or laugh to themselves. Patience is more than a voluntary virtue; it is a way of life for them.

Moses went from "hero to zero"—from being the son of Pharaoh's daughter to the backside of the desert. His self-esteem went from the pinnacle to the pits. Moses came to the place in his life where he learned confidence. His "S" type personality is seen when he was commanded to lead the children of Israel out of Egypt, but he resisted this responsibility.

"S"s are extremely loyal, and they often work with the same company for years. They also tend to be family-oriented and dedicated to their loved ones. Interest in their families is evident by the photos and mementos covering their walls or desks.

"S"s do not like aggression or antagonism. Their strong sense of loyalty, however, compels them to come to the aid of family or friends who are in trouble. They ardently defend them physically and verbally, stepping out of their comfort zone, shocking themselves and others.

They are not interested in showing off in a large group. They tend to seek out personal relationships, talking one-on-one or to a few people at a time. "S"s have the ability to listen for hours about anything. They are "people-people" with the ability to work while they talk or listen.

Calm In The Storm

Athletics brings out the best and worst in people. Tom Landry, former head football coach of the Dallas Cowboys, gives us a lesson in control. I never saw him lose his temper. In fact, the most expressive thing I ever saw him do was extend his arm with a closed fist and whisper, "All right!" after a Super Bowl touchdown. On the other hand, John Madden, former coach of the L. A. Raiders, would run up and down the sideline demonstrating his feelings.

Athletes express their personalities in different ways. "D" football players knock your block off and then growl in your face. "I" players are the ones who invented the end zone dance. (My favorite to watch was "Neon Deion" Sanders .) "S" athletes may knock you silly, but then say they are sorry. "C"s ask lots of questions and execute best when they know exactly what to do.

Competitive sports create elation, pressures, and roller coaster rides all in short periods of time. "S"s seem to handle the challenge better than anyone. Sometimes they handle it too well, and they do not get excited enough.

Calming excited people and making others feel comfortable seems to come naturally to "S"s. They are not high strung, and they usually make great marriage partners and employees because of their concern for a steady and stable environment. They respond calmly to aggression, often defusing problems with their sincere interest and self-controlled temperament. They seek cooperation rather than control. As peacemakers, "S"s are servants who work patiently and persistently to resolve conflicts between people.

Because they have the patience to develop specialized skills, they often learn skills others will not or can not learn. "S"s appreciate routine rather than despise it. Their ability to do the same thing repeatedly makes them specialists. Concentrating on the task at hand is a great strength. Because of their ability to concentrate on getting the job done, they do not easily get bored. Their attitude of persistent service makes them invaluable to employers.

"S"s want high touch, not high tech. They want to support and serve, maintaining the status quo routine because they feel insecure with change. New things, especially high tech things, are threatening to them. They work best under controlled, stable environments. IBM concluded that business owners and managers needed to upgrade their equipment for faster and more efficient productivity, but "S" secretaries resisted. Therefore, IBM designed a commercial that said, "It's okay to get a new typewriter as long as it's an IBM."

"S"s usually do not make a big deal about anything. They do their work well without fanfare. Sincere appreciation and consistency make them happy because they desire an environment which includes security. Safety is imperative, and they shudder at the thought that someone could possibly get hurt. To these safety conscious people, security is the positive product of happy and healthy surroundings.

Do not rearrange the office furniture without giving "S"s ample time to evaluate. They need explanation for changes, and they want time to adapt. They prefer slow alterations and easy turnovers. They like to create stability in their environment, and to preserve that stability.

One of the most important environments to preserve is the home environment. "S"s require minimal work infringement on their home life. They desire 9:00 to 5:00 work schedules, and they want their weekends to be free.

Appreciation Means Everything

I have known many "S"s who generously gave themselves to others. A pastor friend served his church for years. The church had grown slowly but solidly. He had sacrificed his rest, study time, and sometimes his family's needs for the sake of his members. After years of his tireless service, one deacon became antagonistic toward him. This deacon was a "D" who wanted to see more action and growth.

"D"s can be every pastor's dream or nightmare. In this case, the deacon became defiant and disloyal. Eventually the conflict was more than the pastor could stand, so for the sake of his church, the pastor made the ultimate sacrifice and resigned. For him, flight was better than fight.

If the church had been more appreciative of his labor of love, he may have stayed. However, he felt like the church did not appreciate him. "S"s desire credit for the work they do, but they seldom express that need. Although they accomplish many tasks, "S"s are often the unsung heroes. A little credit where credit is due goes a long way with them. They do not get excited about red stars next to their names.

Sincere Appreciation

"S"s respond best to sincere appreciation. They lack high ego strengths, so they often appear to have low self-esteem, and their quiet demeanor is often misunderstood. Their strength is quietly and methodically seeing a job through to completion. "S"s often seek identification with a group. They do not want to dominate or direct, but they need to be a part of a team.

Of course, they tend to become active in serving others, but they also relish the opportunity to develop potential friendships. Their slow responses to pressure make them an asset to any group. "S"s are not self-promoting, though they are self-protective.

In a crowd, they are the silent crusaders. They need leaders who will speak up for them and take up their causes, especially when they are discouraged. "S"s desire someone to defend their feelings and promote their needs—someone to be assertive for them.

Satisfied With The Status-Quo

Detailed procedures are important to "S"s, and they prefer environments where they can consistently operate without confusion. Because of their need for security, they desire limited territory. Familiar, comfortable surroundings give them more confidence.

Their sense of comfort comes from predictable patterns and familiar situations. They often withdraw from new challenges to avoid the risk of failure, they are usually slow to speak, and they appear less active than others. They feel most comfortable with standardized procedures. Without this standardization and simplicity, they may become unsettled and insecure.

"S"s need more organization than explanation. Once procedures are clarified, they can follow them better than the extroverts. They even enjoy the simple tasks that often frustrate others, but everything must be explained and organized for them in a simple and understandable manner.

They need exposure to people who react quickly to the unexpected. Because of their slow responses, they need to build relationships with those who can handle sudden challenges well. By understanding their own apprehension about change, "S"s can adapt to a situation more easily. Reacting quickly is sometimes just as important as reacting smoothly, therefore they can benefit by observing those who respond more quickly to opportunities or difficulties.

"S"s should stretch themselves to meet the challenges of an unexpected task. Their need for stability should not stifle opportunities to serve others. Though they are uncomfortable with change, they can respond to unexpected situations if they understand their natural reluctance. To stretch themselves, they should become involved in more than one thing at a time, not allowing their insecurity in a situation to cause them to withdraw. They are capable of many tasks with the proper scheduling of time and space.

Supervision of "S"s should include constant reinforcement. They usually prefer that others take on new jobs and challenges, but they need to realize their own capabilities and have confidence to tackle new opportunities themselves. They probably can do a lot more by exerting a little more confidence.

Lean On Me

Known as "Flip Phlegmatics," "S"s tend to flip back and forth according to the amount of pressure put on them. Their easygoing nature is so flexible that they may give the impression of having no convictions or strong emotions. Since they seldom respond outwardly to pressure, they provide a welcome balance to bold, outspoken people. They need to become more assertive in unpredictable circumstances.

"S"s need to be more assertive and less sensitive. Rather

than avoiding confrontation, they should learn to respond more assertively. They need to overcome their fear of being intimidated by others.

Since many people are "S"s, situations often arise where there are all Indians and no Chief. When a need arises, someone must take responsibility and assume leadership. Someone needs to become decisive rather than quietly waiting for other people to respond.

The "S"s' greatest weakness is being naive. They have trouble saying, "No!" Everyone knows they will do what no one else wants to do because they care so much about pleasing others.

I personally admire "S" behavior the most because it happens to be my greatest need. I respect their ability to stay calm. Unfortunately, their slow response and laissez faire attitude are often misunderstood as laziness or lack of commitment. They can be misunderstood as being wishy washy, but their loyalty and calm are great strengths. My hat is off to "S"s! May their tribe increase!

Warning

"S"s, however, can be doormats for aggressive, insensitive people. If you are an "S" and live or work with someone who abuses you sexually, physically, emotionally, or verbally, I strongly encourage you to get professional help. You must learn how to be strong for yourself!

Talk to your minister or a counselor, but do not just wish the problem away. It will not go away until you do something about it. Whatever you do, do not try to solve it overnight. You can not just put your foot down and demand that things change. Significant change takes time, planning, and courage.

Assertiveness training courses can help you. Recognize the

fact that your best attribute can potentially become your worst liability. Beware that the strength of being a servant does not become the weakness of subservience. Your desire to serve will generally be supervised by a stronger person, but do not let him or her take advantage of you.

"S"s enjoy relationships with people who contribute to the task at hand. Though they are willing to do it all themselves, they work best as part of a team. Getting input from others adds security to their environment. They are prone to becoming caught up in conversation and neglecting their work, but they are also willing to work all night to accomplish a job, especially if someone else will work with them.

"S"s need co-workers who are flexible in their work procedures. Bosses may demand the task be done their way, but these people often feel that they work better alone and without pressure. They are comfortable when doing the job at their own pace, and others would be wise to give them some flexibility. However, they need to learn to adapt to changing situations. Conditioning them to change increases their productivity. Sometimes the rules change halfway through the game, but that does not mean it is time to stop or slow down.

"S"s must learn to respond more quickly to pressure and be more assertive. The impatience of others bothers them. They are patient themselves, and not quickly frustrated. They feel pressure when instant change is demanded. Immediate action is threatening to them.

Because they believe that others can accomplish tasks faster or better, "S"s need continual reassurance that their contributions are invaluable. Communicating specific, sincere praise to them is imperative because they want to know their work and service are appreciated.

Sources of Conflict

"S"s avoid conflict better than anyone, but they can act just like "D"s when you mess with their family or friends! They can be extremely protective, and they often take up other people's offensives. Like a mother hen, "S"s can attack and react with surprising force. Submissive people resist pushy and bossy people, and they respond best to those who are steady and security-oriented. They do not like challenges. "S"s get nervous when things get hot. Sometimes their craving for stability can make them unstable, and they explode or do crazy things when they are overcome with pressure.

On television, we sometimes see news accounts about employees who have been fired and then return to murder the boss, employees, and even customers. They can not take the stress. Their world crumbles, then they snap. People wonder, "He was such a quiet guy. I can't believe he would ever do such a thing."

"S"s are not the only ones capable of crazy behavior. All people have their buttons and emotional pressure points. When pressed too hard, anyone can break. "S"s, however, repress their feelings. Other personalities seem to be able to express and resolve their emotions better than these security conscious people.

"S"s are irritated by people who are disloyal. They work hard for those who are appreciative and kind to them. They do not seek lots of friends, but they will be faithful to those who prove to be trustworthy. I have seen "S" women who would not hurt a flea, become strong leaders when their families were threatened.

Quiet Mother Turned Maniac

I once saw a quiet, reserved mother become a "maniac on a mission" when the school principal verbally condemned her son. She confronted him with "fire on her breath!" She held nothing back. Her power took everyone by surprise. Afterwards, she was apologetic for her outrage, but she did not need to be. Her response accomplished precisely what she intended, and she got her message across with authority. "S"s can bite your head off, then say they are sorry later. "S"s can be used in great ways, but they often doubt their influence and ability.

"S"s make great parents, teachers, mates, employees, and friends, but they need to be more sure of themselves. Assertiveness training can be helpful. "S"s who desire to be more assertive may benefit from finding a successful business person who will mentor them. "S"s may not be aggressive enough to ask someone for help, but one of the most important things they can do is to ask someone to help them be more assertive.

I once counseled a couple who both had high "S" personalities. Their sixteen year old daughter was a "D" who threatened to run away if her parents did not let her do what she wanted. The child had control of the family. In fact, the roles were reversed: the parents acted like children, and the child acted like the parent. I encouraged the parents to be more firm. Do not give "D" teens an ultimatum such as, "If you don't like it, there's the door!" They will choose the door and devastate the "S" parents.

Instead, give the child choices, and give them opportunities to be responsible. Gradually let the child assume greater responsibility for their choices as they mature. "S"s do not want conflict so they usually give in to the child's demands. It is much more effective to design a compromise that shows your

63

willingness to trust and your determination still to be in control. I know it is not as easy as it sounds, but you should carefully consider how your personality affects your relationships.

Supervising and confronting "S"s at work is much like dealing with family members. They respond best to leaders who are understanding and friendly. They do not like antagonistic environments. Appreciative relationships with others make them feel good about their work environment. Their effectiveness can be increased by working with those of equal competence. They become angry and stifled when superiors constantly correct them. Working with equals with similar attitudes and abilities makes them more productive.

Directions and Guidelines

Give "S"s guidelines for accomplishing a task. As faithful friends and loyal workers, they do not always ask questions. Instead, they make assumptions in order to work quietly on their own. Provide specific directions to enable them to feel secure about the tasks they are accomplishing.

Encourage their creativity. Force them to "step out of their shells" and try something new and daring. Creativity may not come easily for people who would rather follow a prescribed ritual at home or at work, but wonderful experiences and victories are theirs once they learn to be more imaginative.

As natural skeptics, "S"s should strive to be more positive and persuasive. Their demands for safety and security may seem petty and demanding to others. This need for stability discourages them from assertive, risk-taking roles.

"S"s should remember that a lack of friction is not always positive. Pleasing others sometimes is a defense, not a strength.

Of all the temperaments however, people with this temperament will have the fewest enemies and the longest history of effective service.

The ancient story of Queen Esther reminds us how loyal she was to her people. She showed "S" behavior by being willing to die for them. She stated bravely, "If I perish, I perish." She was also very creative. Her tendency toward pessimism was overcome by her faith.

Esther was willing to die for what she believed. She turned her natural weakness into a supernatural strength. Her commitment seemed uncharacteristic of "S"s. She was naturally timid and shy, but her inner strength responded in a surprising way. Her intense love and loyalty made her stand firm, and she was an example to everyone who fears conflict.

Relating To "S"s

"S"s respond best to warmth and friendliness. They do not like to be pushed into anything, so give them time to change. They make wonderful Sunday school teachers, but do not change their room or curriculum half way through the quarter!

They are slow to make friends because they do not initiate relationships. They listen well, but you have to ask them questions to get them to talk. Show genuine interest in their family and friends; be patient and kind. Try to see life as they do, and you will probably enjoy life more. Learn from them — relax, do not attack people, do not fight back, slow down and smell the roses.

Life is more simple to "S"s, but they are not simple people. They may be very talented, but you may never know it because they do not like to show off. Encourage them to share their talents in a small group before asking them to perform in front of a large crowd.

"S"s can have great stories to tell, but they seldom share them. They feel people are not really interested, or they think they can not communicate their stories well enough. A friend once shared her story to a small group of women. She was extremely shy. Just thinking about sharing it just about killed her! Other people can not understand how difficult public speaking can be for others. She felt like she was going to die! She sheepishly shared how God had worked in her life, and everyone was encouraged by her message. She was relieved once it was over. (Her heart started beating again!) This unwilling and fragile woman was used to help others in a mighty way. People overlooked her fear and saw strength through her weakness.

"S"s can have powerful impacts on others once they get past their shyness. They make wonderful friends in times of crisis. "S"s are used in mighty ways when they control their fears, rather than letting their fears control them.

Satisfying The Cautious Personality

I know someone who is never wrong! She is right about just about everything. Every time she is wrong I sing the doxology, but I am beginning to forget the words because I sing it so seldom!

Sometimes she irritates the stew out of me! Once I had enough of her nitpicking, so I confronted her, "You're too pessimistic!"

"I'm not pessimistic," she responded. "I'm realistic."

I thought that was clever, but it was only an excuse for her constant questioning and analysis of everything anyone ever said or did! I also told her, "You worry too much, too!"

She replied calmly, "I don't worry. I just get concerned."

She probably worries (or "gets concerned") too much. "D"s do not worry enough, and it sometimes gets them into trouble. We often take too many risks, but "C"s carefully analyzes things before they take any risk at all.

"C"s are:

- Calculating
- Conservative
- Cautious
- Competent
- Compliant

"C"s promote quality in products or services in existing circumstances. They are task-oriented, passive people. As thinkers and analyzers, they work on solving problems. High tech is more important than high touch to them. They respond to form and function rather than feelings, therefore reasoning rather than relationship drives them.

"C"s pursue perfection and sometimes carry correctness to

67

extremes. They prefer to accomplish one thing correctly than to partially complete ten tasks. They follow directions and standards very carefully, and they want to comply with the rules while stressing quality in their work. They have very high standards, and they concentrate on details. They want to do everything "just right."

"C" teachers may have the most attractive bulletin boards in the entire school, but when they are complimented, they respond, "But look at the upper left hand border. It's a quarter of an inch off!" These picky people pinpoint problems rather than focus on the potential. They are more aware of burdens than blessings. "D"s would say, "Who cares? You got the bulletin board done." "I"s would probably want to borrow it for them to use next quarter. And "S"s would politely ask, "I helped put it up. Can I help you, too?"

Doubting Thomas

"C"s are not easy believers. They need explanations and answers. They often have to analyze the problems before exercising their faith. They work well in controlled environments. They tend to be conservative decision-makers, checking all the options and leaving no loose ends. They need precision and predictability.

"C"s are diplomatic with most people, but they can also be critical. Weighing their words for effectiveness, they may inflict vicious verbal jabs to make their point. Correctness is their greatest concern. They constantly check for accuracy. They tend to be quite competent, but they are only cautiously confident. Accepting a fact at face value is very difficult because they feel compelled to dig deeper or probe further. This level of analyzing can be annoying for others, but in most cases their thoroughness is reassuring.

Because they are not satisfied with surface answers, these calculating people turn over every leaf and read every line. Their inquisitive natures consume them. They need in-depth answers.

Methodical

"C"s tend to become experts in specific areas because they absorb themselves in whatever they do. They criticize freely, no matter if it is their performance or another person's. Seldom is anything ever 100% right in their eyes. With an eye for quality, they strive to better themselves and others. Finding a better way of doing things is their cup of tea.

They are critical thinkers. They ask, "Why?" and tell you if something could be done better. At times, precise thinking makes them too picky. They can be thorns in the flesh because they are naturally pessimistic and find flaws.

As passive individuals, "C"s tend to comply with authority. They are not aggressive when confronted with a challenge. Instead, they try to find a way to fix the problem. They do not desire to be in control for control's sake, but they demand that things be done correctly and in order. They do not respond well to differences.

Complying is easier for them than communicating, and they believe silent surrender is better than open confrontation. However, this often leads them to hold grudges, engraving in granite the memories of past offenses. Forgiving and forgetting are very difficult for them. Known as "Moody Melancholies," they tend to drown themselves in introspective reflection rather than engage in open communication.

Because they question everything, including themselves, these critical, calculating people need to be continually reassured. They focus on problems rather than solutions, and this challenge demands they work in sheltered, stable conditions. The slightest trouble is magnified in their minds, and dealing with more than one problem at a time can be overwhelming for them. "C"s need constant encouragement because they are pessimistic by nature. Their concern for correctness causes them to worry. They seem to doubt more than most.

You may have friends who demonstrated Murphy's Law long before anyone ever heard of Murphy! They think the worst. So-called "C" type friends jump to conclusions, judging and condemning things and others.

Faith and optimism are often foreign to them. It is hard for them to relax when problems exist all around them. Their theme song could easily be Hee Haw's popular tune, "Gloom, despair, agony on me. Deep, dark depression, excessive misery. If it weren't for bad luck, I'd have no luck at all. Gloom, despair and agony on me." Instead, "C"s would do well to sing, "Don't worry! Be happy!"

The need to prove their competence can cause conflicts. I have a friend whose "D" personality clashes with his wife's "C." Sometimes he comes home with a brilliant idea. He wants his wife to bow down and say, "That's a terrific idea! You're so smart! Go for it! Do it!" He will begin to present his thoughts, but halfway through she finds three things wrong with his idea. (He is lucky she stopped at three!) Her response never fails to take the wind right out of his sails. He has trouble dealing with it, but actually he needs her analysis and caution to balance his enthusiasm.

Interestingly, the problems his wife sees are usually very important issues which he needs to consider, and he is embarrassed because he did not think about them first. He once got upset and said, "Why do you have to be so negative? Why do you have to be so fault-finding?"

And she responded, "Why do you have to be so stupid? Why

didn't you see those problems first?"

She is the best thing that has ever happened to him. She forces him to raise his "C" and lower his "D," to think through his exciting ideas and bring them down to earth. Another time he got so angry he said, "You make me so mad I could bite your head off."

She responded, "If you did, you'd have more brains in your stomach than you do in your head." He decided to keep his mouth shut!

Quality Control

"C"s want "SOP"s (standard operating procedures). They dislike uncertainty and want to know exactly when, why, how, where, and what. They are most comfortable when order is valued and confusion is limited. They work best under structured conditions, so consistency is critical. Abrupt alterations threaten them with their biggest emotional challenge: the fear of being incompetent. They think change for no good reason is insane. Others may scurry to test a new possibility, but "C"s drag their feet until convincing facts are presented.

The status quo allows them to refine and improve the system. "Quality control" is their personal motto. If they can not do it right, they do not want to do it at all. They are the perfect fit for the job that requires precision and detail. Because they are never satisfied unless they complete the job right, they are the consumer's best friend because they sincerely desire to do the best job they can.

"C"s take great pride in their work. They are their own worst critics, but they appreciate recognition of their craftsmanship. They do not seek personal praise, but they appreciate attention for their finished product. You may criticize them, but do not criticize their work!

"I"s are very sensitive to personal criticism, but they may not care if someone criticizes their performance. "C"s are just the opposite. They take personal rebuke lightly, but are deeply offended if people dare to criticize their work! They enjoy situations that call attention to their accomplishments. They strive to provide first class products and services, and they prefer opportunities that focus on their projects rather than themselves.

"C"s usually want others to be in charge. Though they are often critical of leadership, they need those who have confidence to make final decisions. Willing and able to give direction, they often hesitate because of their cautious style. These cautious individuals seldom make mistakes because they seldom make decisions!

"C"s who work closely with those in authority offer excellent counsel because they know they will not be ultimately responsible. This often gives them the freedom to be bolder than others.

Focused On The Function

"C"s want to work on solving a particular problem, and they crave the chance to do what others can not do. Typically, they are slow decision-makers, and they can learn from decisive individuals. Instead of wishing they had more time, space, or money to do a better job, they should consider the counsel of superiors and then move ahead. They need to remember that expediency and sufficiency are sometimes best even if it means the quality of the work is a little less than perfect.

"C"s need supervisors who use policies as guidelines, not as threats. Giving them the flexibility and minimal restraints produces maximum results in their work. Limitations may be necessary, however, and they should be open for specific improvements. They want guidance, but they also want the opportunity to do things right.

They often give the impression of being so busy that people feel they can not get close to them. They become more and more disinterested in people as they are absorbed in their projects. Distractions annoy them and produce caustic responses. Written across their faces is, "Don't bother me, I'm busy!"

"C"s are often fussy, but the motivation to look for flaws may be the desire to be superior to everyone else. They are often insensitive to the needs of the people closest to them. Unaware of other people's interests, they seem to drift into "Never Never Land." While searching for a better way, they can lose sight of reality.

My wife tends to asks me questions like, "Why do we park on driveways and drive on parkways? Why is there a permanent press setting on my iron? Why is there an expiration date on sour cream? And why is the Secretary of the Interior involved with everything outdoors?"

My answer is, "I really don't know." And to tell the truth, I really do not care! Understanding the oddities in life are not important to me, but she is perceptive enough to see the inconsistencies in even the little things in life.

In Search Of Excellence

"C"s are not adventurous, but they are inquisitive for quality's sake. Searching for new thrills is not nearly as important as seeking new truth. They need the balance provided by those who will compromise, and they need others to help them find the medium between opposing views. Often unwilling to compromise, they tend to offend others. Because of their natural ability to see problems, they should be careful about open criticism. They need to allow opportunities for others to state their positions. They would be wise to hold back at times and allow someone else to find flaws and make the first response so they are not perceived as being "always negative."

Precise, detail work allows them to be most effective, so they should look for jobs that require them to do what they do best. Working in a supportive environment with broad limitations and specific goals adds to their productivity. They need opportunities for careful planning. Their clarity and objectivity go hand-in-hand. Having time to think, evaluate, and make corrections is important. They deplore disorganization and carelessness. They prefer specific job descriptions, and they like to know exactly what their job requires. Without this clarity, confusion reigns and frustration results.

A Difficult Question

"C"s have an intense need to understand. When my oldest son, Curtis, was five years old, he asked me where God came from. I proceeded to expound: "God is preexistent. He has a quality of life that demands no beginning and no end. He is the Alpha and Omega, the First and the Last, the Almighty and Infinite One." After that scholarly dissertation, my son surprisingly responded, "Oh!" I am sure he was thinking of ten other questions!

Because of their need for explanation, periodic appraisals should be scheduled. They desire feedback and help along the way, and evaluations of their performance from time to time enhances their work. They must learn to respect people as much as they respect their own accomplishments. Because of their strong task-orientation, they tend to get over-involved in projects and forget people, but the value of a person exceeds a completed project.

Developing tolerance for conflict is also a very important

lesson for cautious, compliant "C"s. Their passive personalities cause them to withdraw and verbally hold back. They tend to run away in order to avoid trouble.

Because they are perceived as competent, they often get appointed to committees in the church. People know they don't make quick decisions; they are cautious and careful. I once went to a finance committee meeting carrying a gravy stained napkin with notes of what I wanted the church to do next year. My friend, Cal Robbins, shared later how the gravy stained napkin did not impress him, especially when he noticed the gravy was not dry! He said, "You just jotted those notes at your dinner table before the meeting." He is a "C" and likes to see feasibility studies and validation reports. He was the VP of Human Resources of a large chain of department stores. He was a very effective board member; he definitely was not a "yes man," and I respected his judgment and insights.

From that experience, I learned that board members look at my plans through their unique personality perspectives. "D"s want me to get to the point. They like to see the bottom line. Short and decisive meetings are best. "I"s like to talk a lot and want opportunities to share their feelings. They are very sensitive to the emotional atmosphere in the church.

"S"s are conscious of everyone's personal needs. They are very sensitive to the poor and needy, and they like to see love expressed to everyone. "C"s are the protectors. They scrutinize everything and guard every penny. They are a pain to an aggressive, visionary friend or associate!

I recommend leaders go to board meetings prepared to communicate to every personality type. "D"s respect strong leadership. Have a dream. Be purpose-driven. Set goals. "I"s are impressed with your optimism. Be positive and expressive. Show them you feel strongly about your proposals. "S"s are family-oriented. They are loyal. Be kind and patient. Treat them like you would want someone to treat your mother. Be gentle.

"C"s need lots of explanation and time to change. They need for you to do your homework before you present an idea or plan. Plan your work. Come to board meetings with thick reports relating to whatever you want to discuss. "C"s are often the only ones who will read the report, but at least they will feel that you are prepared.

People Are Part Of The Process

To become more effective, "C"s must remember that conflict is a normal part of life. Burdens can become blessings and opposition can become an opportunity to learn. They are valuable problem-solvers, but they need to improve their people skills.

"C" parents, teachers, mates, and employees can be very difficult to live and work with. They tend to be too task-oriented, and often rub people wrong. Relationships are built on agreements, and people respond best to those who share a common bond. These naturally critical people need to learn to be more agreeable instead of judgmental. They can become very lonely people because few friends will endure their need to be always right.

"C"s often focus on correctness and miss the fellowship and feelings of others. Compromise is important to healthy relationships. Some people take offense at the thought of compromise, but it is absolutely necessary in marriage. "C" partners need to be more tolerant and forgiving. Their moodiness can kill love. Constantly pressing for perfection can discourage anyone. They need to learn to be more positive and optimistic.

Children of "C" parents often feel like they can never please their parents. The children may clean their rooms, but their rooms are never quite clean enough to suit the parent.

At work, "C" supervisors can erode good attitudes by never complimenting their employees. Constant criticism (even if it is accurate) is demotivating. Try focusing on the good your employees do. It will increase their effectiveness.

"C" employees must remember to not complain too much. It makes fellow employees avoid you. It also makes management think you are not a team player, and therefore, your chances for promotions may be affected.

Conflicts

"C"s are "experts," even at conflict. They have perfected their way of finding fault in nearly everything. If there is a flaw in the plan, they will find it. They have the intuitive ability to find the weak spots, but fault-finding is extremely annoying to the dreamers and doers. "D"s inevitably clash with "C"s over implementing an idea. "D"s want to do it immediately, but "C"s want to take more time to research and prepare.

There is so much to learn about harmony and Human Behavior Science. We can be our own worst enemy. Our personality can be a real source of irritation to people. My heart's desire is to be a lover not a fighter, but some times I go too far and become too soft and become a wishy washy, spineless compromiser. I need to be balanced: a man of steel and velvet at the appropriate times.

I am responsible for my responses to challenging situations and difficult people. I am not responsible for their responses. The School of Hard Knocks often uses the death of a vision, broken relationships, failed opportunities, and unfulfilled expectations to teach us great lessons.

An Unforgettable Lesson

I experienced a traumatic situation with my oldest son once. I thought I had to be totally in control of my children. "C" children can be finicky, and our first born was very inquisitive. His persistent questions challenged me. My typical response was, "It's not for you to question but to obey." That worked until he was almost a teenager. One day he asked why he could not do something. I simply said, "Because."

He thought about it for a second. Realizing that was no answer, he responded, "Why, 'because'?" Irritated, I retorted, "Because I say so."

Again he thought for a moment. He still did not understand, and questioned, "Why 'because you say so'?" Sensing defiance, I blurted, "Because I'm your father!"

He paused to think that answer over a little longer, then he concluded he still did not understand, and persisted, "Why 'because you're my father'?"

I was angry (and I did not have the foggiest idea of a good answer), so I yelled, "Go to your room! Do all things without murmuring and disputing!'" But I also bit my lower lip like Ricky Ricardo on the "I Love Lucy" television show. My son began to laugh because I looked so funny.

But I did not think it was funny in the least! I glared at him and slowly growled, "You'll never laugh at me again!" I proceeded to give him a spanking right there. I lost my cool. I never had disciplined him without first explaining why. I always made sure he understood what he had done wrong. I always did it under control . . . but not that day.

He ran to his room crying. I went to my room almost crying. I knew I had blown it. I prayed, "Lord help me understand what just happened. Help me understand myself and my son. What should I do now?"

A few months earlier, I had administered a personality profile to Curtis. I had just been certified as a "Human Behavior Consultant." When I blew up at him, I realized I needed some objectivity, so I looked at his assessment and found he is a "D/C." He is a "D" like I and a "C" like his mother, but I was treating him only like a "D."

I went to his room and said, "Son, I need to tell you something. I think I have been doing you wrong."

He said, "You're absolutely right about that, Dad!" He then said something that really hurt. He sobbed, "You've made my life so miserable for the past six months that sometimes I don't even feel like living any more." I just about died. I wanted to be the perfect father. I hardly missed any of his Little League games. I was always there for him, but something had gone wrong.

I said, "I'm sorry, Curtis." It's hard for "D"s to say they're sorry. I then told him he could laugh at me any time I bit my lower lip. (He's laughed a few times since then.) I also promised, "I will answer your questions. I may not answer them when you ask, or I may not answer them how you want, but I promise to answer your questions."

Our relationship used to be very close. When he was a young boy, he would crawl up into my lap and whisper, "You're my Dad, and I'm your son!" In those six months, our relationship had been strained. After my humbling experience and promise to answer his questions, we began to draw close again.

Several years later, a wonderful thing happened. While attending college, Curtis came home for Thanksgiving break. I was lying on the living room floor watching a football game, and he laid his head on my chest. I was so thrilled to think he felt comfortable enough to be close to me again.

I thought back when he was twelve, how I blew it and learned a tremendous lesson about loving him and answering his questions. I thought about when the apostle John lay on Jesus' breast. I thought of all the fathers who wished their teenagers wanted to be close to them. It was wonderful!

After a while, I needed to get up. I wanted to be funny, so I said, "What am I, your pillow?"

I will never forget his answer. He simply said, "No, you're my Dad." I wept quietly.

Questions, Questions, Questions

"C"s ask questions after questions. It is not that they are not smart. In fact, "C"s tend to be very inquisitive and great learners. They need to guard their constant search for answers and learn how to be happy without understanding everything.

"C"s make great students, if their teachers satisfy their quest for knowledge and understanding. "C"s need to avoid against becoming moody, if their search is not being satisfied. We should be content, no matter what state we are in.

"C"s make the most competent, yet often most challenging people to work and live with.

The following is a simple drama that could take place in any classroom.

Rocky, Sparky, Susie, and Claire

To illustrate the importance of understanding others, picture a teacher asking his or her class the simple question, "Who discovered America?" There are all different types of personalities in the class.

Rocky, the high "D" yells out, "Columbus. Next question!"

The teacher responds, "Why did you yell out like that, Rocky? Why don't you raise your hand like everyone else?"

Rocky likes to take charge. He wants to be in control. He wants to get everything done in a hurry so he can go play.

The teacher asks again, "Who discovered America?" Sparky, the high "I" jumps up, waving his hand, and says, "I know, I know. Call on me, teacher! Please!"

She responds, "Okay, Sparky, who discovered America?"

He acts like he knows, but says, "Oh, I forgot. It's right on the tip of my tongue. Can you give me the first letter?"

He wants to turn it into a game like Wheel Of Fortune. He asks, "Can I buy a vowel?"

The teacher sighs, "Oh Sparky, put your hand down and stop acting like a clown. Why do you always raise your hand without having anything say?"

Sparky responds with a surprised silly face and sits down while the class laughs at his antics.

The teacher then asks Susie, the high "S", "Who do you think discovered America?"

Softly Susie says, "I think it's Columbus, but I'm not sure. If anyone else knows and wants to say, it's okay with me. And if you don't like Columbus, I'm sorry. I hope this doesn't make anyone mad."

Finally, the teacher asks Claire, the high "C", "Do you know who discovered America?"

Claire gives the teacher one of those disgusting glares and blurts out, "Now what do you mean by that question?"

Rocky explodes, "Come on, Claire! Why do you make a mountain out of a molehill. Let's finish this nonsense so we can go play!"

Rocky loves recess. He considers himself King of the Playground. He tells everybody, "We're going to play kickball today. I'm captain." And pointing to a friend, says, "And you're captain of the other team."

Another strong-willed student interrupts, "I don't want to play kickball. And who made you captain anyway?"

That is a "D" challenging another "D." (That is how you start new businesses!)

Sparky gets all excited. He says, "I love it when Rocky is about to get into a fight." Sparky yells, "Ding, round two," like the ring announcer at a boxing match.

Poor Susie covers her face and begins to cry. Sobbing she says, "I'm sorry. I'm sorry. I didn't know it was going to upset everyone. Please forgive me and don't fight."

Finally Claire screams, "Now wait a minute! What about the native American Indians? They were here before Columbus. What about the Vikings? They were also here before Columbus. You need to be more clear with your question!"

Every individual responded according to his or her personality. Each one had a predictable pattern of behavior. This is an age-old truth with very modern applications. Understanding DISC personallity types often explains why people do what they do!

Point #3

Applying the 4 temperaments to daily activities can be simple and practical!

If identifying one out of four different personality types was all we had to do, then personality profiling would be easy. The challenge comes from recognizing there are many blends and combinations of temperament types.

We do not want to dig so deep that we possibly miss the practical lessons in personality profiling. The following is a brief overview of the different behavioral blends and the enlightening practical applications we can learn from identifying them.

There should be a time when personality theory turns into practical application. Putting feet on what you learn must turn into wise daily decisions that make you more effective when working with people. You should not only identify obvious personality types, but also look for the blends and composite behaviors that go deeper and wider as you improve your people skills.

Once you have identified your primary personality type, you should look for your behavioral blend. Most people have two and sometimes even three personality tendencies influencing their personality. Having one specific type makes interpreting and applying your personality to life's challenges easier.

Since most people have two types influencing their behavior, it is important to understand the numerous behavioral blends. These blends will help explain the dichotomies and oxymorons that may confuse us and others. These strange bedfellows are normal, but sometimes uncommon. Looking at them from a practical perspective can be extremely enlightening.

Behavioral Blends

Everyone is endowed with a unique personality. Our pre-birth personality development begins to take form even before our first breath. Our parents, environment, and early childhood experiences continue to shape our unique personalities and we become the products of many influences which touch our young lives.

When you have two or three behavioral types evident in your composite personality, you are simply revealing that you can have more than one motivation influencing your actions, thoughts, and feelings. This could indicate that you have a healthy understanding of the uniqueness of your personality and that you know how to manage it.

Fifteen percent of people have only one primary DISC personality type. Eighty-five percent of people have a secondary type. In fact, most people have a blend or composite of behaviors, and they have a combination of two or more motivations.

You probably have a specific behavior blend — a combination

of motivations that influences your feelings, thoughts, and actions. This, however, has nothing to do with Multiple Personality Syndrome. It simply means that people have normal combinations of influences, which affect the way they behave.

Behavioral blends *are not* like schizophrenia, either. There are normal combinations of personality types and there are abnormal types. Schizophrenia is caused by chemical imbalances and "short circuits" in the brain. The behavioral blends we are going to identify are normal and natural. Some are more prevalent than others, but all are evident in the lives of every normal person.

Multiple Personality Syndrome

Interestingly, after I conducted a seminar at the awesome Saddleback Community Church for Pastor Rick Warren, I had a woman call me a few days later to say she had been diagnosed with MPS (Multiple Personality Syndrome). She said she had four distinct personality types and that she just did my personality profile as each of her different personalities.

She was amazed to find that she had all four (DISC) personality types affecting her often unusual behavior. After she got off the phone, I told my wife, "That was easy: no matter what I told her, I was right!" I was taking insensitive liberties, joking about a very serious subject, but it seemed funny at the time.

Since then I have come to understand better the tremendous pain some people have with MPS. It is a serious problem and can not be written off as "craziness" or pure "demon possession." People with multiple personalities often have other influences, but I have found that many, including very religious people, have clinically explainable problems.

Discovering that you have a behavior blend is not a clinical or abnormal situation. It is perfectly natural to have one, two, and even three DISC behavior types affecting why you do what you do.

To identify your behavioral blend, or composite behavior, find the definitions that best describe you.

As you do this, you will begin to understand your composite behavior. At the same time, you will learn how two or more types influence your personal motivations. This is not bad. It is not abnormal. It will simply explain how you may be affected by different feelings, thoughts, and desired actions at the same time.

Review the following pages with your personality type in mind. See what lessons you can learn from studying your behavioral blend. Also study the other blends. Notice how there are many different composites of the four basic personality types. Our personalities are composites of four identifiable temperaments. No blend is better than the other. Each blend simply describes the complexity of our personalities. Only 15% of people have a predominant "D" or "I" or "S" or "C" personality. The other 85% have a mixture of two or three specific types. A few examples are:

• "D/I" • "S/C" • "I/S" • "D/C" • "I/C" • "D/S," or • "I/S/C"

There are actually 256 possible composites, but we will focus on twenty-one behavioral blends. There is tremendous diversity in nature. There are many different kinds of animals, stars, and people. There are 150 or so different kinds of dogs, but they are all canines. Each breed of dog is different, yet they are similar in many ways. In the same way, there are many different kinds of behavior, but they are all part of the complexity of human personalities.

Pressure and stress reveal what we are made of: our temperaments as well as our character. Adversity has a way of demonstrating and refining our personalities. Just as fire and heat temper steel, our problems can strengthen us. Each behavioral blend has its unique ways of responding or reacting to pressure.

Adversity is like the clay in the potter's hand. The potter carefully applies pressure to mold the clay into a vessel. In the same way, life has a way of using stress and problems to mold us.

Overview of Behavioral Blends

Study the brief paragraph descriptions in this section. You may be a combination of two specific profiles. You can also have some characteristics of other types, but usually, people fit into one or two behavioral blends. Each set of descriptions begins with a brief summary of the single, unblended personality type which is followed by blends of that type.

Dr. John Geier, who developed the original Performax Personal Profile System, originally identified 18 blends which he called "Classical Patterns." His research concluded that these patterns were the most common blends. Since that time, Dr. Geier has added three more patterns which are blends of three types. Please note: there are two "D/I"s but no "D/S." The two are included because there are two distinct varieties of this blend, and the "D/S" is omitted because these people are described in the "S/D" blend.

D: "Determined Doers"

"D"s are dominant and demanding, and they want to win at all costs. They do not care about what people think; they want to get the job done! They are insensitive to others' feelings. They are determined to get going, but they need to be more attentive to details. They are motivated by serious challenges to accomplish tasks.

D/I: "Driving Influencers"

"D/I"s are bottom line people. They are much like Dynamic Influencers (see next paragraph), but Driving Influencers are more determined and less inspirational. They are strong doers and able to encourage others to follow. They need to be more cautious and steady. They often get involved in too many projects, so they need to slow down and focus on one thing at a time. They are motivated by opportunities to accomplish great tasks through a lot of people.

D/I (lower): "Dynamic Influencers"

"D/I"s are impressive and demanding. They get excited about accomplishing tasks and looking good. Determined and driven, they influence large crowds best. They can be too strong and too concerned about what others think. They have good communication skills and are interested in people, but they need to be more sensitive and patient with the feelings of others. Slowing down and thinking through projects are crucial. They are motivated by opportunities to control and impress.

D/C: "Driven and Competent"

"D/C"s are determined students or defiant critics. They want to be in charge while they collect information to accomplish tasks. They care more about getting a job done and doing it right than what others think or feel. They drive themselves and others, and they are dominant and caustic. Improving their people skills is important, and they need to be more sensitive and understanding. They are motivated by choices and challenges to do well.

I: "Inspirational Influencers"

"I"s are impressive people. They are active and excited individuals. Approval is important to them. They can have lots of friends if they do not overwhelm people with their enthusiasm. They can be sensitive and emotional, but they need to be more interested in others and willing to listen. They do not like research unless it makes them look good. They often do things to please the crowd because they are entertainers. They need to control their feelings and think more logically. They often outshine others and are motivated by recognition.

I/D: "Inspirational Doers"

"I/D"s are super salespeople. They love large groups. They are impressive and can easily influence people. They need a lot of recognition, and they often exaggerate and talk too much. They jump into things without thinking them through, so they need to be more studious, reflective, and cautious. They are motivated by exciting opportunities to do difficult things. If they are not careful, they live to please the crowd and get themselves into trouble. They make inspiring and determined leaders.

I/S: "Inspirational Specialists"

"I/S"s are influential and stable. They love people and people love them. They like to please and serve others, but they do not like time controls or difficult tasks. They want to look good and encourage others, but they often lack organizational skills. They follow directions and do what they are told, but they should be more concerned about what to do, than with whom to do it. They are motivated by interaction and sincere opportunities to help others. Whether they are up front or behind the scenes, they like to influence and support others. They make good friends and obedient workers.

I/C: "Inspirational and Competent"

"I/C"s are inspiring yet cautious. They size up situations and comply with the rules in order to look good. They are adept at figuring out ways to do things better through a lot of people, but they can be too persuasive and too concerned about winning. They are often impatient and critical, and they need to be more sensitive to individual feelings even though they are very sensitive about what others think of them. They do not like breaking the rules, and they do not enjoy taking risks. They need to try new things and sometimes go against the crowd. They are careful communicators.

S: "Steady Specialists"

"S"s are stable and shy, and they do not like changes. They enjoy pleasing people and can perform repetitive tasks. Secure, non-threatening surroundings are important to them. They make good friends because they are so forgiving, but other people sometimes take advantage of them. They need to be stronger and learn how to say, "No." Talking in front of large crowds is usually difficult for them. They are motivated by opportunities to help others.

S/I: "Steady Influencers"

"S/I"s are sensitive and inspirational. They have lots of friends because they are tolerant and forgiving. They do not hurt people's feelings and can be very influential, but they need to be more task-oriented. They need to learn to finish their work and do it well. They like to talk and should pay more attention to instructions. They are kind and considerate, but they would be more influential if they were more aggressive and careful. Motivated by opportunities to share and shine, they readily induce others to follow them.

S/D: "Steady Doers"

"S/D"s get the job done. They prefer stable surroundings and are determined to accomplish tasks. As quiet leaders, they relate best to small groups. They do not like to talk in front of large crowds, but they want to control them. They enjoy secure relationships, but too often try to dominate people. They are motivated by sincere challenges that allow them to accomplish tasks systematically. They make good friends even though they have a driving desire to succeed.

S/C: "Steady and Competent"

"S/C"s are stable and contemplative people. They like to research and discover the facts, and they like to weigh the evidence and proceed slowly to a logical conclusion. They enjoy small groups of people, but they do not like speaking in front of large crowds. They are systematic and sensitive to the needs of others, but they can also be critical and caustic. They are loyal friends but can be too fault-finding. They need to work on their enthusiasm and optimism. They are motivated by kindness and by opportunities to accomplish tasks slowly and correctly.

C: "Cautious Competent"

"C"s are logical and analytical. Their predominant drive is careful, calculating, compliant, and correct behavior. When they feel frustrated, they may withdraw in despair, or in contrast, they may become hyperactive. They need others to answer their questions patiently. They are not sensitive to the feelings of others, and they can be critical and crabby. They prefer quality and reject phoniness in others. They are motivated by explanations and projects that stimulate their thinking.

C/S: "Competent Specialists"

"C/S"s have to be right. They like to do one thing at a time and do it right the first time. Their steady and stable approach to things makes them reserved and cautious. They are consistent and careful, but seldom take risks or try new things. They do not like speaking to large crowds but will work hard behind the scenes to help groups stay on track. They are motivated by opportunities to serve others and to do things correctly.

C/I/S: "Competent, Influencing Specialists"

"C/I/S"s like to do things right, impress others, and stabilize situations. They are not aggressive or pushy people. They enjoy both large and small crowds. They are good with people and do quality work. They are sensitive to what others think about them and their work. They need to be more determined and dominant. They can do things well, but are slow in decision-making. They are capable of doing great things through people, but they need to be more self-motivated and assertive. They are stimulated by sincere, enthusiastic approval and logical explanations.

C/S/D: "Competent, Steady Doers"

"C/S/D"s are a combination of cautious, stable, and determined types of people. They are task-oriented, but they care about people on an individual basis. They do not like to speak in front of crowds. They prefer to get the job done—and done right—through small groups instead of large groups. They tend to be serious and are often misunderstood by others as being insensitive. "C/S/D" types really care for people, but they just do not show it openly. They need to be more positive and enthusiastic. Natural achievers, they need to be kind and considerate, but they would be more influential if they were more aggressive and careful. Motivated by opportunities to share and shine, they readily induce others to follow them.

I/D/S (or any combination of D, I, and S): "Inspiring, Driving, and Submissive"

"I/D/S"s are impressive, demanding, and stable. They are not as cautious and calculating as those with greater "C" tendencies. They are fairly active, but they are sensitive and steady. They seem to be people-oriented, but they can be dominant and decisive in their task-orientation. They need to be more contemplative and conservative. Taking charge and working with people are more important to them than details.

D/I/C (or any combination of D, I, and C): "Dominant, Inspiring, and Cautious"

"D/I/C"s are demanding, impressive, and competent. They tend to be task-oriented, but they are comfortable before crowds. They need to increase their sensitivity to others. They do not mind change. Active and outgoing, they are also compliant and cautious. They like to do things correctly, but they also influence others to follow because their verbal skills combine with their determination and competence. Security is not as important to them as looking good.

Straight Mid-Line

A Straight Mid-Line Blend occurs when all four plotting points on the DISC assessment are in the middle area of the graph. This may indicate that the person is trying to please everyone. Striving to be "all things to all people" may be a mature response to pressure, or it may show that the person is experiencing intense frustration. When this person takes the profile, they may answer in ways they thinks others want them to answer instead of stating their real thoughts and preferences. They can complete another profile several months later to get a more accurate reading.

Above Mid-Line

Some patterns indicate unique struggles an individual may be having. An Above Mid-Line Blend occurs when all four plotting points are above the mid-line. This may indicate the person feels compelled to over-achieve.

Below Mid-Line

A Below Mid-Line Blend occurs when all four plotting points are below the mid-line. This may indicate that the person feels insecure and is not really sure how to respond to challenges.

We should constantly examine ourselves in order to improve our effectiveness and relationships. It is always better to judge ourselves, rather than have someone else judge us. Even though judging others is wrong, people do it all the time.

If we periodically take inventory of our behavior, as well as listen closely to those we love and those who love us about how we tend to respond — especially under pressure — we will be much better off.

There are often several factors and influences that affect us. Therefore, understanding and controlling our behavioral blends can help us correct and improve our actions and reactions.

The following are simple, but practical insights for controlling your behavioral blend.

Controlling Your Behavioral Blend/s

When we discover our personality types, we can recognize the specific areas in which we need to improve. The following are admonitions and challenges to help you focus on becoming more balanced. These points apply to all of us, but they are especially pertinent in our areas of weakness and need.

D: "Determined Doers"
- Be careful to not offend people when you take charge.
- Anger is a normal human emotion, but it must be controlled.
- Pursue purity and peace.
- Focus on doing one thing well.
- Be kind to everyone, because everyone is carrying a burden.

D/I: "Driving Influencers"
- Though naturally fearless and able, you need to respect others.
- Guard the overuse of your strengths; be nice to others.
- Making peace is a greater challenge than winning a fight.
- Choose your words carefully.
- Control your feelings.

D/I (lower): "Dynamic Influencers"
- Develop humility and obedience.
- Remember everyone has a boss, even you.
- Avoid rebellion.
- Recognize that winning is not always most important.
- Be patient with others.
- Rely on others instead of your ability to make things happen.

D/C: "Driven and Competent"
- Seek to get along with everyone.
- Be kind and loving.
- Show more love.
- Seek to serve, not to be served, and have a "servant's heart."
- Recognize meekness is not weakness.
- Control your desire for power over others.
- Take time to be still.

I: "Inspirational Influencers"
- Do not exalt yourself.
- Listen more.
- Work at being organized.
- Concentrate on doing what is most important.
- Prepare thoroughly.
- Be careful what you desire.
- Do not be overconfident, and watch what you promise.

I/D: "Inspirational Doers"
- Guard the power of your words.
- Do not use flowery language just to impress people.
- Always tell the truth.
- Be small in your own eyes and attitudes.
- Give others the glory for all you do.
- Put others before yourself.
- Beware of the "lust of the flesh and pride of life."

I/S: "Inspirational Specialists"
- Beware of always seeking everyone's approval.
- Seek to please others and make them look good.
- Be more task-oriented.

- Do not be lazy.
- Work hard.
- Do not just talk about what you want.
- Be industrious.

I/C: "Inspirational and Competent"
- Do not think too highly of yourself.
- Be a good example.
- Care more about insignificant people.
- Be bold and confident.
- Guard what you say.
- Do not flatter yourself.

S: "Steady Specialists"
- Increase your confidence.
- Fear not.
- Speak out more often.
- Be outgoing and less inhibited.
- Be assertive.
- Do not be insecure.

S/I: "Steady Influencers"
- Think things through.
- Take stands.
- Guard against fearfulness.
- Remember, you do not always need people to encourage you.
- Always do right and take charge if you have to.
- Prepare more.

S/D: "Steady Doers"
- Let people know you are capable and confident.
- Speak out.
- Be excited.
- Be strong in your weaknesses.
- Encourage and help others daily.
- Reason and evaluate more.

S/C: "Steady and Competent"
- Be assertive and strong.
- Be more enthusiastic.
- Enjoy relationships rather than endure them.
- Peace and happiness do not come from security and safety.
- Deep peace is knowing there are answers to your problems.
- Be fearless.

C: "Cautious and Competent"
- Be more patient when you correct others.
- Correct others in love.
- Be more positive.
- Hope in the possibilities, not your circumstances.
- Build relationships with others.
- Find happiness apart from fulfilling your tasks.

C/S: "Competent Specialists"
- Think more positively.
- Guard against the fear of failure.
- Focus on the possible.
- Be cheerful.
- When everything is going wrong, be encouraging.

- Take more risks and be assertive.

C/I/S (or any combination of I, S, and C): "Competent, Influencing Specialists"

- Guard against being judgmental.
- Avoid bitterness and resentment.
- Step out of your comfort zone.
- Be thankful for everything.
- Be encouraging and a good example to others.
- Take charge and do whatever you need to do.

C/S/D (or any combination of D, S, and C): "Competent, Steady Doers"

- Be more enthusiastic.
- Do not worry so much about problems.
- Be more positive.
- Be more sensitive.
- Do not be reluctant to lead because of poor verbal skills.
- Be more outwardly optimistic and encouraging to others.

I/D/S (or any combination of D, I, and S): "Inspiring, Driving, and Submissive"

- Be more calculating and careful.
- Be more organized.
- Be careful what you promise.
- Give others the glory for all you do.
- Think before you act.
- Be humble and slow to speak.

D/I/C (or any combination of D, I, and C): "Dominant, Inspiring, and Cautious"

- Listen more.
- Be more sensitive to other's feelings.
- Be a peacemaker.
- Do not be judgmental.
- Be optimistic and encouraging to others.

Straight Mid-Line

- Recognize your importance.
- Relax more.
- Remember you cannot please everyone all the time.

Above Mid-Line

- An Above Mid-Line Blend may mean you are trying too hard to over-achieve.
- You may feel pressure from unrealistic expectations.
- Stop attempting to do so much.

Below Mid-Line

- A Below Mid-Line Blend may indicate you feel threatened or insignificant.
- Let others encourage and guide you.
- Be more optimistic and think better of yourself.

Applying what we learn is the next level of profiling. It really does not matter how much we know about personality types. It is what we do about it and how it helps us be more effective that matters most. The following are some general applications that should be practiced.

General Practical Application

High "D"s

- They need challenges and choices.
- They do not like to be told what to do.
- They want to be their own bosses.
- Controlling themselves is most important.
- Desiring to control others, they must first control themselves.
- "D"s need to guard their feelings.

Since "D"s test and challenge authority, they need to learn that everyone has a boss. If not, they will push others to the limit. Instead of telling "D"s to complete a task immediately, give them the choice between completing the task now or by a certain time. They will usually choose the latter, but they at least have the choice.

High "I"s

- They need lots of recognition, approval and stroking.
- They like to talk and get attention.
- Being quiet is difficult for them.
- Give them opportunities to express themselves.
- Do not put them down for their desire to entertain.
- Encourage them to control their excitement and share the limelight with others.

"I"s need to learn they will have more friends when they make others look good. Praise them when they do well. Emphasize how their poor behavior makes them look bad, when they underachieve. They especially need to guard against pleasing everyone.

High "S"s

- They desire steady and stable environments. Change is difficult. Give them time to adjust.
- Do not expect them to accept risks or try new things. They prefer traditional roles.
- Difficult assignments and enthusiastic challenges are not effective. Friendly and sweet appeals are best.
- Encourage "S"s to be more outgoing and assertive, so that they will not be taken advantage.

"S"s' natural submission causes others to take advantage of them. "S"s need to learn how to control their reluctance to be bold and assertive. Saying "no" can be frightening, yet powerful. Taking chances and risks to take charge can be very rewarding.

High "C"s

- They like to do things right. Finishing a project half way or half right is unacceptable to them.
- Give them time and resources to do their best.
- Do not push them to always do better. They may get frustrated and give up.
- Encourage them to improve their people skills. They need to learn to be more sociable.

Answer their questions and explain the "whys of life." Provide these types with happy and positive atmospheres. They tend to be naturally pessimistic and moody. Joyful and uplifting music around the home or office can be very encouraging. Avoid being constantly negative and critical, especially with these personality types.

Extensive Practical Application

Each of us needs specific, practical applications to enhance our strengths and avoid our weaknesses. The following pages contain general suggestions to help people with each personality type.

Seeing our behavior in others can help us understand ourselves. By recognizing the "quirks" of those around us, we can improve our own behavior. Often, the things we dislike in others are the very things we struggle with in our own lives. An ancient proverb applies this principle to marriage teaching us to "Dwell with 'our wives' according to knowledge." How do we do this?

I dwell with my Honda according to knowledge because I know when to change the oil, rotate the tires, and give the car a tune up. I know how to make my Honda operate at maximum efficiency.

When I married, I knew very little about my wife. In fact, I knew very little about dwelling with anyone according to knowledge. I did not know why others did what they did—what made them tick. I had a lot to learn about living and working with people. I became a student of my wife, her needs, her moods, her desires, and her behavior. Every day I learn more and that knowledge helps me respond more appropriately to her.

Wisdom That Works

Practical application is making knowledge work. If we do not know how to use knowledge, it is worthless. Being people smart is knowing why people do what they do, but being personality wise is knowing what to do about it. The tragedy in most relationships is that people do not even have the basic knowledge of human behavior. Understanding how and why we are the way we are is important, but practical application is what makes our knowledge power-ful. After all is said and done, we need to apply what we learn. The goal is to apply truth in our specific areas of improvement. Life is a journey toward maturity. We are always improving but never arrive at a place where we can not learn more. It is a challenge, plus an adventure that should be a steady and reasonable journey.

Did you notice that I used D, I, S, and C terms in the last sentence? "D"s respond to challenges. "I"s love the adventure. "S"s desire steady and stable emphasis, and "C"s look for the reasonable things. We respond to life according to our personalities. Practical application helps us recognize our strengths and weak-nesses so that we use our strengths wisely and overcome our weak-nesses. Some of the greatest lessons come from on-the-job train-ing. All the books and seminars in the world can never compare to the lessons we learn from life's experiences.

Experience is a great teacher. The problem is we often fail to learn from our experiences. Someone has said, "The only thing we learn from history is that we don't learn from history." We have learned that people respond in many different ways. We respond according to our own personalities, but each person we meet with has his or her own personality, and the clash of different tempera-ments causes conflict.

Volumes have been written about human behavior, but wisdom is attained only by *using* the knowledge we acquire. Learning pro-vides knowledge, but wisdom provides practical application.

Practical Application for "D"s

"D"s must learn how to be team players. Their desire to be in charge tempts them to fly solo. Although they may be able to do some things better by themselves, they can be more influential

104

as part of a team. We should seek to strive together in peace, but working with others can be difficult. Driven people can make life difficult, because they tend to take control and constantly want to push ahead. They need to train themselves to include others in their decision-making. They also need to be aware of the needs and drives of others.

Working with "D"s who refuse to play second fiddle to anyone can be exasperating. Often they do not understand their emotions and actions. They can benefit from a clear explanation of why they have such determination.

Choices, Not Commands

"D"s do not like being told what to do, so it is important to give them choices. Instead of telling a "D" employee that they must get the job done by 9:00, give them a choice between 8:30 or 9:00. Ask them, "Which one do you want?"

Explain who the boss is, and teach them responsibility by allowing them to make some decisions for themselves. Make sure they realize that there are consequences if they do not act responsibly. Get "D" employees to agree beforehand on the consequences they will face if they do not do as they say they will.

A wise religious leader once said: "Choose you this day whom you will serve!" "D"s love straightforward confrontation. "D" leaders often feel compelled to challenge everyone. When they control themselves, dominant leaders are very effective. But when out of control, they can be disastrous.

Do not let "D"s intimidate you. They need parameters for their behavior and actions. They stretch the limits, so you must let them know how far is too far. They desperately need good role models for self-control. Show them how to stay in control by remaining calm while dealing with them.

Meekness Is Not Weakness

"D"s should be taught that meekness is not weakness. The strongest people who ever lived were meek. Meekness is power under control. The harder it is to stay in control, the more important meekness will be. Seneca, a Roman philosopher, wrote that meekness was "the disease of the soul." With the backdrop of this thinking, Jesus dropped the bomb of meekness on the Roman world.

Anyone can lose their composure, but the meek can control their anger. Anyone can blow his or her top, but those who are truly meek are able to control their feelings and actions. "D"s who struggle with anger should literally walk away from an explosive situation. They should not do what comes naturally—what they feel like doing at the moment. Chances are, that is the worst thing they could do! An ancient proverb states, "You should not strive or be pushy, but be gentle." The word "strive" can mean "to war, to quarrel, to fight."

Driven, determined people are most effective and influential when they are not threatened. Do not push them! They tend to respond like wild animals that have been cornered. They attack! Give them a way out by giving them a choice or negotiating a settlement in which they are able to save face and not feel intimidated.

"D"s Under Authority

"D"s must learn to respect authority figures such as the police, teachers, and bosses, even though these people seem to make life difficult. They do not enjoy being submissive. There is something in them that cries for independence and wants freedom, but the worst bondage is enslavement to one's own emotions and actions. True freedom comes through being under authority.

We cannot truly possess authority until we learn to submit to authority. The most powerful people in the world are under some type of authority. When they learn to work in healthy dependence on others instead of defiant independence, they will be more successful.

"D"s typically see submission as weak or cowardly, but this can be used as a tremendous opportunity to show them what strength under control really means. They lose their authority if they lose the respect of others. Then they have no platform to influence people. Understanding the principle of respect for authority is imperative for them.

Showing Feelings

"D"s also need to learn how to show their emotions without blowing their tops. Their short fuses get them into trouble. When faced with opposition, people must choose between reacting and responding. There is a big difference! Responding is measured and controlled; it is based on wisdom. Reacting is saying whatever comes off the top of your head in spite of its effects on others. Reacting is lighting dynamite; responding defuses it. When you respond rather than react, you remain in control. Learning to respond properly is perhaps the greatest challenge for "D"s.

Showing feelings of warmth and kindness is difficult for demanding, dominant people. They see crying as a sign of weakness. Expressing your feelings is allowing yourself to be transparent with others.

Crushed Through Crisis

Most "D"s have not ever been broken. They are so full of themselves that they can lose their effectiveness in helping others. They want to control everyone and everything but have not learned to control themselves. (I know. I have learned this through my own experiences.)

Crises teach them to be humble. Once they realize they are not as infallible and powerful as they thought, "D"s become broken. Out of that brokenness comes a more sensitive attitude toward others. Like in a hurricane, there is an eye or calm in every crisis.

Going through the trials of life with this perspective makes the storms easier to bear. Crisis has a way of bringing even the toughest people down to size. "D"s can turn a crisis into a challenge by controlling themselves.

Practical Application for "I"s

"I"s are driven by their strong desire to impress and influence others. They want to be recognized for their accomplishments because rewards are important to them. Speak positively about them in public. Employers would be wise to recognize how pleased they are about their employees' accomplishments. Everyone deserves this, but these "I" types thrive on personal recognition.

"I"s like to look good. I remember once opening the back door of our home and shouting to the entire neighborhood, "I want everyone to know how proud I am of my son." He just stood there with a big grin on his face. Another time, I pretended to call the President of the United States and tell him how wonderful my son was. He knew I was only pretending, but he still loved my show of attention.

The "I"s Have It

"I"s enjoy excitement—the more enthusiasm, the better! Some employers may really have to work hard to get excited, but it pays off for an "I" employee. An ancient proverb encourages us, "Whatsoever you do, do it heartily." That means to do things with enthusiasm. "I"s love this, but those working with them often think they overdo it. "I"s long for group activities. They do not like to work alone; they need frequent interaction with others.

Some bosses can not take much noise, so they avoid having their employees in their offices for any length of time. Leaders of "I" types should work with their individual needs privately. Find ways the employees can work without so much noise and confusion. "I" individuals need the opportunity to inspire and impress others.

Understand that these types may get overly excited. They tend to be too enthusiastic, which makes their leaders avoid group activities. But remember, these employees need more socialization than others, and it will benefit them to be involved in group activities.

"I"s need opportunities to express themselves. Asking them to obey without allowing them to question or share their feelings can be frustrating for them. It is not that they are questioning authority; they simply need to talk when they feel pressure.

"I"s will even talk themselves into doing what they resisted. Do not try to "out talk" them. Wait patiently and listen until they are ready for your response. That may never happen, so ask them to let you talk when they are finished.

They will probably interrupt you and take off on another long-winded discourse. Again, wait for a while and then remind them you never finished. This may happen several times, but each time you are building a stronger case for them to learn they need to improve their listening skills.

They Talk Too Much

Once they realize how patient you have been (and how inconsiderate they have been), you will have enough time to share your thoughts. They probably will not listen well, but it will make them think. This process helps "I"s to understand what you are trying to say.

It is usually a good idea to ask "I"s to share what they think you have just said to them. Do not condemn them for not listening if they get it wrong. Simply question yourself for possibly not making your words clear enough, and then rephrase your statement. Give them another chance to explain what you are saying until you both come to an agreement about the conversation.
"I"s are good talkers but poor listeners. An ancient proverb teaches, "Let every man be quick to hear, slow to speak, slow to wrath." That is great advice for everyone, but "I"s especially need to learn how to be slow to speak and quick to hear.

"I"s need to learn how to share the limelight. They are usually talented, and they love to show off, but they may have a problem with pride and an intense desire for others to notice them. Help them overcome this tendency by complimenting their ability to handle losing or by explaining how impressed you are when they are willing to play second fiddle. It takes a big person to allow others to receive the credit he may deserve.

"I"s would be wise to remember who they serve. They are often enamored by their own talents and abilities, and they love to be praised by others. Their desire for notoriety and significance affects their feelings and actions. Their drive to inspire and influence others is often motivated by a desire to feel important. This motivation gets them into a lot of trouble! They need to evaluate why they do what they do.

Disciplined Feelings

"I"s need to learn how to reflect and prepare. Those who are "I" type students have the potential to make excellent grades, but they sometimes fail because they socialize too much. They do not like to miss any of the action anywhere!

Bosses can use the "I" employee's desire to impress others as a means of encouraging him or her to reach their goals. Reward them with the kind of things that will improve results. Also, use incentives which motivates them to achieve.

Find creative training methods to relieve them from sitting still for long periods. Get them to listen in shorter intervals, ten or fifteen minutes at a time, and encourage them to tell you what they have learned. Invite them to communicate it back in their own words. This may test your patience as a leader, but it could be exactly the motivation the "I"s need to succeed.

These enthusiastic, energetic types do not like to sit still. They are active, people-oriented and love to impress others. "I"s have the ability to outshine most others. They are naturally the center of attention. The problem comes when they live primarily to get that attention.

Practical Application for "S"s

"S"s respond best to kind, thoughtful people. Avoid raising your voice or losing your temper with them. They need to be in secure, calm environments to function at their best. A wise saying teaches, "A soft answer turns away wrath." This is applicable for everyone, but "S"s have mastered the art.

They do not like intense or loud behavior, but seem to be the most patient. They back away from unstable situations and unsettling challenges. They are not risk-takers and are not comfortable around aggressive people. If possible, avoid putting them on the spot.

"S"s do not become easily excited. They may sometimes seem to be disinterested or bored, but it is simply their steady nature to appear so. They are likely to become your best friends because of their sense of undying loyalty. They will stand by you and help you in any way they can.

Time To Recover

Give "S"s plenty of time to adjust. They prefer slow and gradual changes and need time to respond without being pushed. They do not like surprises. If you know there is going to be a change, warn them far enough in advance so they can prepare for it. They usually are not resistant people, but they will be less than enthusiastic if they are not given enough space and time to adapt to change.

High touch is important to them, and they want to feel like a part of the family. Greet them by hugging or grasping their hand with both of yours. Everyone needs intimacy, but "S"s respond the best to a warm and sincere touch.

People-oriented individuals must learn to guard against being naive. They tend to be manipulated by others because of their kind and gentle demeanor, and one of the most important things "S"s need to learn is how to say "No." They tend to agree to do everything people ask them to do. They are vulnerable; people take advantage of them.

Assertiveness training is a practical help. As difficult as they may find it, they *can* learn to stand strong. Their love for people and sense of loyalty make them easy prey for opportunistic, unscrupulous individuals. They need to be cautious and ask questions before they trust others. "S"s should not feel guilty for saying "No" or worry that they may have hurt people or let the group down. Someone else can do the task they declined.

Don't Work Harder. Think Smarter.

"S"s need to learn how to turn a request for help into an opportunity to challenge others. They can be more assertive and stimulate others to take more responsibility. They can be bold enough to challenge a "D" to volunteer, enthusiastic enough to stimulate an "I" to get involved, and convincing enough to get a "C" to respond. Leadership is the "S"s' most difficult task, but they can be excellent leaders if they learn to be assertive.

Because they cringe at the thought of pioneering, they should become involved in projects that stretch their "comfort zone." Learning how to adapt and respond to new stresses can be helpful. They have the potential to turn into turtles, retreating into their shells to protect themselves from the possibility of being bruised and bumped. Taking a public speaking course may be the ultimate challenge for them. The thought of getting up in front of people and speaking may be terrifying, but this experience can result in tremendous growth.

Moses must have felt unqualified to lead the children of Israel out of Egypt because he believed his ability to speak was deficient. His "S" type behavior affected his attitude.

Most of the "S"s' problems stem from poor self-assuredness. Reading books and listening to cassettes about self-worth and positive thinking can be beneficial to them. Robert McGee, Zig Ziglar, and James Dobson are the best teachers I know on the subject. Their books can be found in major bookstores. Also, it may be inspirational to read biographies of great leaders who felt inferior but went on to do great things.

"S"s should be more assertive about improving their skills, but at the same time, they need to be careful concerning the philosophy that places one's self in the power center of life. My biggest concern about the science of human behavior is the focus it places on the created rather than the Creator. We should think highly of ourselves, but should not make ourselves the center of life.

I heard a famous lady put it this way, "God don't make no junk!" We are fearfully and wonderfully made in the image of our Creator. We should also improve and grow with confidence. Like the caterpillar in the cocoon, we can strive to become the butterfly we were created to be.

Poor Attitudes

Many people see themselves in a poor light. They believe they are hopeless and shameful, but the reality is that we are loved, forgiven, and accepted individuals. We have hope and a new identity! We need to focus on all we can be and stretch our wings. We need to expand our emotions and actions outside our personal comfort zones and learn how to fly. Fear cripples "S"s. They often refuse to try new things or take advantage of new opportunities simply because they are afraid.

We have not been given the spirit of fear. "S"s need to rise above their emotions to experience the satisfaction of meeting challenges. Instead of refusing a challenge completely, take small steps. Do not be pushed into big challenges. For example, instead of setting a final goal for weight loss, determine an amount per week and eventually reach the goal.

The fear of failure coupled with the fear of the unknown is more than most "S"s want to tackle. By eliminating their mountain of fear and replacing it with rolling hills of desire, they can deal with anything. By focusing on the possibilities and not concentrating on their own weakness, these normally shy people can do anything anyone else can do.

Practical Application for "C"s

The best advice for "C"s is to be willing to settle for less than perfection. Their constant inquiries can be nerve racking; their need for answers causes stress in their relationships. Recognizing their need to fully understand will help others cope with their inquisitiveness. Ask: "Why do you ask, 'Why?'?" This question forces them to think through their question and perhaps answer it for themselves.

As mortals, we will never know everything. We see through a foggy glass and cannot understand all the mysteries of life.

Know-It-All's

"C"s usually are not disrespectful when they question. They just want explanations. Their drive to comprehend causes them to appear rebellious. Actually, they just want to go by the book. But if they do not understand, they can be negative and condemning.

Stimulate them to think through situations on their own and allow them to use their initiative to be competent. Reason goes a long way with them, but typically, explanations create more questions for them to ask. Patience is a great virtue in dealing with them.

They tend to be more task-oriented than other people. Feelings are not as important to them, so they may say or do things that seem to be cold and uncaring. Do not try to appeal to their emotions. Appeal to reason. Recognize that they tend to be moody when they are deep in thought. They usually are not mad or upset; they just act like it! Give them some room. They may misunderstand and demonstrate confusion by expressing displeasure.

Stinging Words

These naturally critical people can be very caustic. Under pressure "C"s can shoot straight, however, they avoid conflict whenever possible. When they feel threatened, they attack. They say what they think, and think about what they say, so they are often right on target. This characteristic of "telling it like it is" often gets them into trouble because most people do not like to hear the truth. "C" types need to learn how to speak the truth in love and season their speech with sensitivity.

The tongue is small but powerful. It is very hard to tame. Constant criticism and fault-finding damage people, and a negative attitude is an insult. You ought to be the most encouraging and positive person around.

Because "C"s tend to worry more than others, it is important that they be surrounded by optimistic people. Do not concern them with problems. They have a knack for finding problems without our showing them! True joy is not found in understanding every-thing or having an answer for everything. We are to pursue truth, but settling the questions of life is not our responsibility. Correct-ness should not be our main concern.

"C"s can be party poopers. They dump cold water on a hot idea faster than anyone, but what they say is often very insightful. It is important to learn to listen to their advice even though they may be critical and negative. Be careful not to miss their wisdom because you do not like their attitude. Others' responses to their concerns affect their participation. Many sit and stew, contributing nothing because they were criticized for being negative.

They need to be more positive. Occasionally they need to search for the pot of gold at the end of the rainbow instead of finding the pitfalls along the way. They should whistle, sing, smile more, and they will see how much better life can be. "C"s should think more about the possibilities. They need to guard their thoughts.

I can imagine them thinking right now, "How corny! How absolutely ridiculous!" That is exactly what I mean. Their initial response is usually negative. They can take this advice and improve the quality of their lives and the lives of those around them who are tired of their gloom and despair.

These critical, observant people are usually accurate in their negative appraisals, but most people do not want friends who are always right! They want friends who will forgive and forget; friends who pick each other up, not tear each other down.

Developing People Skills

"C"s can develop their social skills by becoming involved in social activities or taking up a hobby that involves others. Finding activities which force them to relate and express their feelings will help them to become more sensitive. Above all, they should avoid their natural tendency toward depression by learning to control their feelings of inadequacy or incompetence. They need to relax and learn how to enjoy life. They do not always have to understand or explain everything.

These cautious people tend to be very competent, but they do not care much about friendships. They are not people-oriented, but some of them feel very lonely. Perhaps a lack of friends is the result of being too negative and critical of others. To have friends, we must be friendly. "C"s need to develop their people skills. If they do, "C"s can be the best friends anyone could have because they will always tell the truth. They are not fakes.

They can be difficult people to love, but they can also provide brilliant insights which build up instead of tear down. Their greatest challenge is to be more sensitive and tolerant of others. "C"s should be competent and comforting, cautious and kind, careful and considerate of others.

Understanding our personalities is only half the knowledge we need to learn. There is also a lot of practical application to why we do what we do. Applying it in order to develop ourleadership skills will determine our level of success in life.

Point #4

Leadership often succeeds or fails based on how you control your personality!

A Case Study on Leadership

In 2002 I had just returned from an advisory board meeting in St. Louis. My wife and I were invited to be on this board because we were one of the company's largest distributors out of more than 5,000. With over 300 million dollar a year in sales, this company was starving for leadership training.

There are many great leaders in the field of independent distributors, but the loudest cry I heard all weekend was the need for leadership training from the company. My interest in leadership training and involvement with this company is not a coincidence. I have been researching the subject of leadership for many years and have finally decided to transcribe some of my notes lest I forget these many valuable lessons about leadership.

I sincerely believe this company is the best health-oriented company in the world, but it is not the biggest. I often wondered why. I now believe there was a vacuum of leadership at the top, as well as leadership training to its members. Notice, I did not say there was a lack of leadership overall.

I am continually impressed with the tremendous amount of leadership among the Master Coordinators in this company, but transferring and passing on that leadership ability was what I have found lacking. Perhaps it is because so many people who want to build their own businesses do not have the skills or do not consider themselves as leaders. Or it could be that the leadership at the top had crippled that for many years the leadership growth down through the ranks.

This is not about how to be a great leader, but more on how to get started and how to enhance one's basic leadership skills. I sincerely believe everyone can become a leader. I do not believe people are "born leaders." I believe everyone has the capacity to be made leaders. People learn to lead! It does not come naturally to most people.

There are far more people who would rather follow than lead. They are more comfortable being told what to do, rather than telling others what to do. I am convinced that anyone can become a leader with the proper training and mentoring.

An Interesting Observation

During the summer of 2002 while attending this company's *International Leadership Convention* with some 2,000 people, I listened closely to as many people as possible. Many were already leaders because they earned the right to come to the convention at the company's expense. A few represented the Home Office. They were the most interesting.

Often in a large organization what you hear from the Home Office does not always fit with what you hear from the field, especially when the company has not grown much in the previous ten years. The quality of the products and integrity of the company have improved year after year. I honestly believe that there is no better research and development, plus the products are superior to anything else on the market today.

So why has the company not grown like it should? I can not really address the infrastructure that involves production, marketing, and management. But I can address the one part of the business that I understand well. I know first hand how we in the field responded to all the recent changes and challenges.

One of the biggest needs is for "leadership by example," as well as improved communications. As a human behavior scientist, I am especially concerned for all companies that struggle with leadership and communication. It is the backbone of growth. Without communication, wars are lost, companies fail, and families are destroyed. How we lead and communicate are the vital elements of our success in life.

I have become convinced that how we communicate makes or breaks us as leaders. It is not everything, but it is something leaders cannot avoid. We can become leaders without good communication skills, but we cannot become great leaders without great

121

communication skills.

Communication Is King

A good example is what I observed about the (now "former") president of our company. At first, it seemed he had what it would take to lead this company to become the number one health products company in the world. He came to the company with great experience. I am not sure if he had ever been the president of such a large company.

I am sure he sincerely tried to do his best, but he may have fallen into the pit of the Peter Principal. It simply states that in a hierarchically structured administration, people tend to be promoted up to their "level of incompetence." I will not say that he was incompetent. He was a fair communicator and seemed to know what he was doing, but the company did not grow.

In St. Louis (2002), he was introduced to the Master Coordinators / Distributors by the head legal counsel. She described the company as "a ship stuck in the mud" for the past 10 years. She encouraged us to follow him. We welcomed him with anticipation for what he was about to say, but there was skepticism in the air.

Doubt had crept into many of the distributors of this company because constant changes were taking place. So many of us were anxious to hear what was going to be done to turn this company around. I was a new Master Coordinator and learning quickly that all things were not well.

Trouble Brewing

My concern began that summer when I attended the *International Convention* in Hawaii. The closing banquet featured several speakers from the field. A couple of them were especially not happy with the many changes taking place. They expressed their displeasure openly. I was terribly embarrassed for those, like myself, who had special guests at the banquet.

My son, sister, and brother-in-law had come with us to Hawaii for the convention, all at the company's expense, which my wife and I had earned. They were not familiar with much about the company, but were very impressed that we had earned their way to attend absolutely free. No other company in the world had such a great convention program for its top achievers.

Ironically I was sitting next to one of the speakers. She was very respected and had built a successful organization. She spoke with passion, but also with grave concern. I had mixed emotions. I was confused, because most people up till this night had been so outwardly positive. The cat was now out of the bag. All was not well in Tinseltown.

At the end of the banquet, I thought the president would say a word, but there was nothing. I learned later that he was furious over what had happened. I also learned that a couple superstars had declined an opportunity to speak. I wondered why. Discontentment had come to the top. Confidence looked like it was beginning to unravel.

I thought back to the president's opening and welcoming remarks at the convention. They were serious, but ended with "You have a choice." This was a typical strong admonishment to those who may have been discontented to make up their minds. In other words, it sounded a little like, get-in-or get-out, an ultimatum from the boss.

I overlooked it and rather enjoyed his "challenge" because that is my personality preference. I like strong leadership. I liked what I heard. But I also filed it away in my researching mind for review later. Little did I realize that the future review would come so soon.

Less than two months later in St. Louis I remembered the challenge, "You have a choice!" It seems many of the Master Coordinators were choosing to challenge his leadership. He seemed defensive. I heard he had originally decided not to address the entire group, but instead to only speak to the newly elected officers of the Advisory Board. That really bothered me. I did not understand why.

I learned there was resentment because certain masters had so strongly opposed him. Only after the new president of the advisory board had convinced him to speak did he address our group. It was short, but again very revealing to me, a human behavior specialist.

Our president started very well with good humor and warmth, but then the hint that something was wrong crept out. He challenged the crowd to come to him with suggestions, but not with emotions. He would only reason with the facts, nothing more. He was resistant to anything that resembled "feelings over fact." That was okay, but it was too defensive, so I began to ask a lot more questions.

Most everyone I spoke to shared a common interest in where the company was going. Few seemed to really know. Everyone shared the same goal to lead the company forward, but there was so much uncertainty. Many of the changes were still in the air. Still unresolved. Still undefined. What would the final outcome be? What was the company going to become? The prospects seemed doubtful. Things seemed to be going backwards. That president has since resigned. I wish him well. It is hard being a leader of a multimillion dollar company with thousands of distributors.

I honestly believe success often goes back to the way things are communicated or not communicated. Someone has said, "Everything rises and falls on leadership." I also believe "leadership rises and falls on behavior and communication." And behavior and communication rises and falls on how we are designed and developed as leaders.

Two Years Later

Two years have passed since I first wrote the preceding thoughts. Last April, 2004, I just returned from a special Master Coordinator's Retreat at Half Moon Bay in San Francisco. Oh, what a difference new and better leadership can make. The company had just been purchased by a young, but proven entrepreneur.

He invited all the Master Coordinator Teams to meet him at his expense. I watched and studied intently. This Harvard MBA was much younger (39 years old) than all the other presidents I have seen come and go over the years. But his wisdom was far beyond his years.

He addressed us with the passion of Teddy Roosevelt, yet comforted us with the compassion of Florence Nightingale. He reminded me of what Carl Sandberg wrote about Abraham Lincoln. He was a "man of steel and velvet."

We felt his determination and zeal to lead the company to become a $5 billion a year in sales industry leader in the next ten years, but we saw first-hand his love for his immediate family, plus his care for each one of us as his new extended family. He reminded me of a man of "blue denim and lace." He had the durability of blue denim and the delicateness of lace.

I wrote in my notes last year, "the jury is still out for what the future holds, but as far as I'm concerned, if this guy is for real, you ain't seen nothing yet."

A year has now passed since that exciting weekend at Half Moon Bay when we met our new owner and CEO. I have watched and listened to him closely on several occasions. I have tried to identify through his words and actions his specific personality type. I hate to admit it, because I am supposed to be an expert at reading people, but I can not identify his type. He exhibits all the good personality traits. He is one of the most balanced leaders I have ever met or seen.

This book is for all those, like my wife and me, in great companies who will hang in there for the long haul no matter what. This is especially written to those in the headquarters or working with the public who are struggling with the future. Like all companies, the challenges will first be fought in the command center, then in the field. What the company does will affect what those working with the public do. We *do* have a choice.

We will learn to lead by design or we will destroy all that is important to us. Leadership is a process, not an end in itself. We continually grow as leaders. Once we think we have arrived, we often plant our own seeds of destruction. The fall from the top begins with a small slip. It starts with a little miscommunication. It ends in a war of words where no one wins. We must learn how to lead by design if we are to save "a ship stuck in the mud." Everyone can do it! Everyone is gifted to lead!

Society and human nature often make people feel as though they are not gifted. Some may doubt the idea that they are special, but this is not true. Actually, everyone is gifted. You may not feel special, but you ARE unique!

Your UQ!

Everyone knows what IQ (Intelligent Quotient) means — the higher the better. Understanding our EI (Emotional Intelligence) or EQ (Emotional Quotient) is also important. How we respond emotionally is measurable and sometimes more important than knowing our IQ. Recognizing how we respond emotionally is vital.

I want to introduce a new quotient, UQ — Unique Quotient. Our UQ focuses on how we understand our uniqueness. It is not an actual paper assessment, but it is recognizing that people are not "junk." Even though no one is perfect, everyone can improve their behavior by understanding they ARE unique.

Without a doubt, many people suffer from poor self-images. Somewhere along the line, they have believed a lie and thought that they have not been gifted to do anything special. This idea of being gifted is difficult for them to accept. Beginning early in life, we are influenced by the idea that some people are special and others are not. However, regardless of IQ, EI, EQ or special abilities, every person needs to understand that he or she is uniquely special.

Identifying our natural motivations and giftedness helps us feel better about ourselves. But this does not mean that we are "sufficient unto ourselves." No matter how gifted we may be, we should always remember that life demands that we be responsible for our actions and care for others.

My Personal Story

I am embarressed to share with you that I almost did not graduate from Miami Senior High School in 1962 because I nearly failed English. I could hardly read and my grammar was terrible. My excuse was that I learned how to speak Spanish before I spoke English. Looking back, it is easy to see that I was going to have problems.

On my first grade report card, my teacher noted: "Mels doesn't pay attention in class, nor does he follow directions." My last report card of that first year said, "Mels is going to have problems in second grade." And I did, plus I had problems in the third and fourth grades and right on down the line. In fact, sifting through the evidence, it is easy to see that from a human standpoint I was not much of an academic type.

My potential overcame my problems.

The point I want to make is that while I am not much of an English scholar, I have not let that cripple me. In fact, here I am writing this book. I am a good example of how the so-called "weak" things of this world can turn their shortcomings into strengths. The same can be true of your life.

I really want to encourage you — especially if you feel poorly about yourself or think that you are not gifted — to take time to think on the possibilities. I do not believe I could have ever written any of my resources if I had accepted my lack of abilities as finalities. Writing and publishing have been extremely challenging for me, but I honestly believe I have been blessed because of my perseverance. Anyone can do just about anything he or she seriously believes. Is there a challenge that you have been hesitant to try? So what's your point?

You *are* unique and gifted to fulfill your mission in life. The question now is what kind of leader will you be?

Are You a Transactional or Transformational Leader? What's the difference?

According to many authorities on leadership there are "two fundamental types of leaders: the transactional and the transformational leader. Transactional leaders engage in an exchange process with followers: 'If you do this, I'll give you that.' Transformational leadership, by contrast, gets people to do far more than they themselves expect they can do."

Transactional leadership is more contingent upon rewards. There is a contract to exchange rewards for tasks. There are promises of rewards for good performance. Accomplishments are recognized. There is a transaction between the leader and the follower.

On the other hand, transformational leadership is inspirational. It provides vision and purpose. Followers are offered something more than rewards. There is a relationship based upon healthy pride, respect, and trust, rather than just accomplishments and rewards.

Transformational leaders have charisma. They communicate high expectations that transform followers and organizations. These types of leaders often overcome the problems that arise from the misunderstanding about leadership. Regardless of what type of leader you are, understanding the science of leadership is imperative.

Everything rises or falls on leadership!

Leadership is the backbone — the heart and soul, the hands and feet that make things work best. Without good leadership, an organization is like a ship without a rudder. It is like an airplane without wings, or like an archer without arrows. Leadership is vital for success, but transformational leadership is more than just leading.

Transformational leadership is a life-long process of "becoming" — of being transformed, in order to transform others. It is not natural traits enabling them to be better than others. People can learn and grow into more effective leaders.

According to Bass and Stogdill, there is "devastating evidence" against the traits theory of leadership. "A person does not become a leader by virtue of the possession of some combination of traits, but the pattern of personal characteristics of the leader must bear some relevant relationship to the characteristics, activities, and goals of the followers."

Most people believe — Leaders are not born.
They are actually made!
But it is probably more accurate to say —
Everyone is born with the innate
ability to become a leader!

Anyone can become a leader. That is what Transformational Leadership is all about: being transformed by the renewing of your mind to become what you were designed to be. Becoming a Transformational Leader begins by recognizing you are endowed to succeed in life. Fulfilling that purpose can transform you into a blended (DISC) Servant Leader!

The most effective leaders are the Transformational Servant Leaders. They are those who understand themselves and others to work on a higher plain of life. They discover the insights that transcend the norm or typical. They learn how and what it takes to impact others.

Understanding Human Behavior Science and applying what you learn can help you identify your style of leadership. Let me encourage you to complete the *Uniquely You Personality Questionnaire* which identifies your DISC temperament type.

You can then simply adapt what you learn to leadership from a Servant Leader perspective. The interpretation and practical application throughout this profile will help you clearly see the relationship between personality types and Transformational Servant Leadership. To complete your profile online go to: *www.uniquelyyou.net* and click on **"Professionals / Leaders."**

Hopefully your assessment will result in better attitudes, improved relationships, and measurable results. Identifying your DISC profile can be the beginning of a new way of leading for you and others. It can make the difference between happiness and sorrow, and between success and failure in life. This profile can help you discover and develop the unique leader within you! It has helped nearly a million people, many of whom were wandering through the maze of life never knowing who they really were or where they were going.

Who Moved My Cheese

While reading *Who Moved My Cheese* by Spencer Johnson, M.D., I began thinking of the main characters — "Sniff," "Scurry," "Hem," and "Haw" from a Four Temperament Model of Human Behavior perspective.

Each one seemed to exhibit specific personality traits. Individually, they had obvious predictable patterns of behavior. Uniquely, each one stood out from the others. Their differences created simple but powerful lessons concerning change and success in life.

If you have not read the book, *Who Moved My Cheese*? or are not familiar with the characters in the book, you may want to skip this section. I do recommend that you read the book, because there are tremendous insights you can learn from a humorous perspective.

Let us recognize each character in the book from their personality perspective. We should also review the four temperament model of human behavior and see what we can learn from these two little people and two mice as they navigate through the maze of life.

The four main characters in the book see and do things from four different perspectives. Some people are active and outgoing, while others are more passive and reserved. Some are more risk-taking, while others are more withdrawn.

If you are familiar with the characters, ironically, most people are Hem types. They are more security and stability-oriented. They do not like taking risks. They do not like change. They prefer the status quo. They avoid challenges and are not really aggressive.

But in defense of Hem, they also make the most loyal friends and employees. They tend to be more sweet, soft, and sensitive than others. They demonstrate many positive, as well as some negative, personality traits.

There is so much we can learn from each character. Hem seems to be the "ugly duckling" who finally comes around. But Sniff, Scurry, and Haw types also have a lot to learn. Let us not jump to conclusions and focus on Hem's faults. Every personality type can act just like Hem at times.

Sniff and Scurry seem to be more positive and optimistic, while Hem and Haw are more negative and pessimistic. Sniff and Scurry act much like extroverts. Sniff is more task-oriented and aggressive, while Scurry is more emotional and enthusiastic.

Hem and Haw are more introvertive. Hem is obviously the most laid back, while Haw worries a lot. This is not to imply that extroverts are better than introverts. We often regard extroverts above introverts. *Who Moved My Cheese* seems to demonstrate the best of the extrovert's traits in Sniff and Scurry and the worst of the introverts's traits in Hem and Haw.

Who has the best personality?

I want to make perfectly clear that extroverts do not have better personalities than introverts. There is a place for passive behavior. To stop and smell the roses is not a bad thing to do. Slow and cautious behavior has its benefits.

I do not believe that Sniff and Scurry are any better than Hem and Haw as far as their individual personalities go. The book's lesson focuses on behavior and how it affects change. When it came to change, Sniff and Scurry are more outgoing and active in their behavior, while Hem and Haw are obviously less active. Sniff and Scurry make better choices than Hem and Haw, but that does not make them better individuals.

We often judge people for better or worse, on how they see a glass of liquid "half full" or "half empty." Everyone sees things through his or her personality type. We have a unique way of looking at change that affects why we do what we do — personally and professionally. Identifying the "uniquely you" is so important. It often makes the difference in how we respond to life's challenges.

Just like Sniff, Scurry, Hem, and Haw, we seem to deal with difficulty through our predictable patterns of behavior. This is not bad, but understanding it can help us not get lost in the mazes of life.

We need to see ourselves in these four characters to find our "strengths" and "uniquenesses." Everyone is divinely designed to enjoy life. You are wonderfully and naturally endowed to succeed in life. Fulfilling that purpose involves understanding yourself and others. Learning how to relate wisely to others is vital!

By understanding why we do what we do, we can improve our effectiveness, quality of life, and relationships. Most problems are pure "people problems." They are misunderstandings of how people think, feel, and act the way they do.

The Science of Human Behavior helps us understand these challenges. Everyone has a unique personality that is neither good nor bad. It is what we do with our personality that really matters.

We must learn how to control our feelings to help and influence others. Managing and supervising others demands that we know them well. Selling and servicing the public requires that we adapt our personalities to those we serve. Helping others begins by understanding their feelings and motivations.

Ironically, many people resist our help. They just do not understand our motives. By identifying unique personality types we can discover why people respond the way they do. We can also learn how to sincerely influence them to accept our help.

Convincing the greatest skeptics involves understanding their motivations. Once we answer their objections, they often become our supporters. Effectiveness begins with insights into peoples' drives. Success results when we learn how to control our uniquenesses.

Leadership Insights

Most everyone responds to life's challenges and choices according to his or her personality. Therefore, individuals who relate to others must be personality wise. For example, High "S" leaders should not engage High "D" followers in small talk. "D"s prefer leaders who get-to-the-point. They want "bottom line" answers. They respond best to those who are not going to waste their time. On the other hand, High "S" followers feel comfortable with leaders who are systematic, slower, and steady in their approaches. "S"s do not like fast talking, quick pace responses. "S"s respond best to stable and sensitive leaders.

Leader Styles

The following section describes different leadership styles. People tend to lead according to their personalities, rather than adapt to the styles of others.

"D" Leaders

"D"s are "take control and be in charge" types. They do not like people telling them what to do. "D" leaders can be too pushy and forceful. They need to control their direct and demanding approach to management. They make better leaders when they learn to slow down, be gentle, and not so demanding of others.

"I" Leaders

"I"s are inspiring and enthusiastic. They love to lead and influence others. Naturally great presenters, they tend to talk too much. "I" leaders need to listen more and not be so sensitive to rejection. They are the most impressive and positive leaders. "I"s love crowds, but need to be interested in individuals.

"S" Leaders

"S"s are the sweet, steady and stable leaders. They seldom demand anything. They are friendly and loyal, but tend to be too nice. They need to be more aggressive and assertive. Overly sensitive to their shortcomings, "S"s need to be more confident. They hate to take risks. They often miss opportunities because of their caution. Reliable and relaxed, they are more reserved.

"C" Leaders

"C"s are competent and compliant. They go by the book and want to do everything just right. They are thorough and detail-oriented, but tend to be too informative. "C"s need to be more positive and enthusiastic. They answer questions people are not asking. When optimistic, "C"s are extremely influential. They should not concentrate on problems, but focus on potentials.

Follower Styles

People also follow according to their personalities. Identifying individual followers' styles make leaders more effective.

"D" Followers

"D"s respect strong leaders. They want to be part of a winning team. They follow with power and authority in mind. They wonder, "Will this action make me more respected and / or get the job done?" "D" followers need choices, rather than "get-in or get-out" ultimatums. They need opportunities to do their own thing.

"I" Followers

"I"s follow with their hearts. They tend to be impulsive followers. They want opportunities that will make them look good. "I" followers talk a lot. They make great first impressions. Their high egos and ability to persuade often turn them into the leaders in order to rise to the top. Sometimes you do not know who is leading whom.

"S" Followers

"S" followers do not make quick decisions. They like leaders who are understanding and gentle. They want to establish a relationship with a leader who will be around for a long time. "S"s are concerned about service and stability. When it comes to sensible and slow judgment, "S" followers feel right at home. They like familiar and low-key environments.

"C" Followers

"C"s are "Consumer Report" type followers. They analyze each decision. They love research and development. "C"s are quality oriented followers. They do not like quick or costly decisions. Picky and precise, they follow with their minds, rather than their hearts. "C"s seldom respond positively at first. They often want time to think about their decisions. Once convinced, they follow best.

The most effective Leader is the blended Servant Leader

These type individuals learn how to adapt and become "all things to all people." They understand that everyone is often motivated by their specific personality. They guard their strengths from overuses, and improve their "uniquenesses / weaknesses."

Blended Servant Leaders control their drives, passions, and wills in order to motivate others more wisely. Servant Leaders are Transformational Leaders who raise people up to follow on a higher plain. Anyone can be a Blended Servant Leader.

Leadership Reflections

Learning about your personality from the evaluations of others can be very enlightening. One way to do this is known as "360 Feedback." By asking 5 or more of your friends and / or associates to complete a *Uniquely You Personality Questionnaire* on yourself, you can learn what others think about your leadership skills.

You may purchase individual 2 page paper questionnaires from *Uniquely You Resources* (phone 1-800-501-0490), or go to: *www.uniquelyyou.com* to order online (a nearly 100 page report). Also contrast your individual personal DISC profile to those you choose to complete a "360 Feedback" on you to compare your profile to the average of what the others assessed.

You may also direct people to: www.uyprofilerBiz.com to complete their individual questionnaires on your DISC leadership styles. Then study the differences and develop strategies to adapt your personal profile to your role as a leader.

Once you have your DISC graphs completed, you can now review the differences between two people's personality types.

Example:

The person with the solid line has a "D/I" personal profile, while his or her leadership role with a dotted line calls for a "S/C" type. One profile is not better than the other. Both profiles have their strengths and "uniqueness."

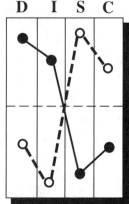

To improve your effectiveness as a leader, notice the differences between the two profiles.

Leaders often struggle because their personal profiles do not match their leadership roles. If the solid line is your personal profile, you may be more decisive or need to be in charge. But your leadership role may know that total freedom is not possible. You must adapt your personal profile to your leadership role profile.

But your "D/I" personal profile may be exactly what your leadership role requires. The "D/I" may want to do his or her own thing, while the "S/C" role as a leader may want to be more cautious. The "D/I" profile wants to be more aggressive, while the "S/C" role as a leader needs to be more reserved.

The "S/C" leadership role needs to be more assertive in order to control your "D/I" natural drives. The "S/C" role as a leader also needs to be aware of the "D/I" personal profile needing more opportunity to "run with the ball." These types are natural self-starters, but will need to guard their aggressiveness and be more slow and soft.

On the other hand, "D/I" roles as leaders must control themselves first, if they want to control their followers. "S/C" leadership roles must always remember certain personalities are control-oriented and need to be instantly addressed. Followers will gain more freedom and responsibility when they learn to obey, rather than resist strong "D" type leaders.

If you have completed your profile, notice all "D," "I," "S," and "C" differences in your contrasting graphs above in respect to your role as a leader and your personal profile. Concentrate on all the DISC letters. Evaluate each letter with your specific role as a leader in mind.

Leadership Intensity Factors

Becoming the most effective leader for a specific task will obviously make a difference between success and failure as a leader. Adapting your personal profile to a specific role is imperative. The following are examples and explanations of how to adapt your natural personality type to your role as a Blended (DISC) Servant Leader.

Stress occurs in every job. The level of pressure can be directly related to your personality in relation to your demands as a leader. In other words, aggressive leaders can cause more stress to the passive and reserved type followers. "D" and "I" type personalities are more suited to active type leaders, but must learn to adapt to the more passive type followers. At the same time, "S" leaders can also be successful as they control their natural reluctance and discipline themselves to be more outgoing. Their style will be "steady, stable and sensitive," emphasizing service and security (trust) as they lead others whether they are active or passive types.

The following are three common opposite types.

Graph A compares a High "I" individual to a High "S" role. "I"s are active/people-oriented personalities. They make great leaders. "I"s tend to not like details. They need to work on time management and call for commitments. They do not like to pressure people. If an "I" were to have a "S" type role as a leader, he or she may become

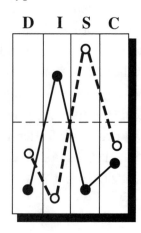

frustrated and bored. "I"s need to be active, working with large groups of people. They love to express themselves. "I"s need opportunities to shine, while "S" roles may require working behind the scenes.

A. "I" Relating To "S" Role.
- "I"s are outgoing, while "S" roles need steady responses.
- "I"s are more optimistic, while "S" roles need sensibility.
- "S" roles require caution, not risks.
- "I"s love to talk; "S" roles may require better listening skills.

Graph B compares a High "D/C" employee to a High "I/S" role. "D/C"s are task-oriented. They love the challenge of completing a difficult task and getting it done right. "D/C"s are not socially active. They prefer telling people what to do and making sure it gets done competently. "D/C"s make good managers as leaders, but need to work on being more sensitive and encouraging to those who work under them. "D/C" roles require more social skills.

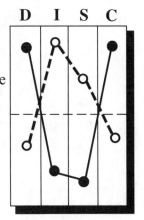

B. "D/C" Relating To "I/S" Role.
- "D/C"s are task-oriented; while "I/S" roles require people skills.
- "D/C"s want to get the job done, while "I/S" jobs need more sensitivity.
- "I/S" roles focus on more service than "D/C"s may prefer.

Graph C compares a High "I/S/C" individual to a High "D" role. An "I/S/C" leader will like to deal with the public and is concerned about the details. "D" roles desire to not get bogged down with details or have to socialize. "D" roles also require a thick skin and decisive leader. "I/S/C"s who have learned to be more "shakers and movers" can handle the role, but may struggle with strong-willed and demanding people. "D" roles may need someone less tolerant and compromising.

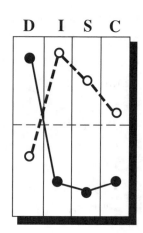

C. "I/S/C" Relating To "D" Role.
• "I/S/C"s are not dominant.
• They prefer socialization and competence in their role.
• "D" roles require aggressive and assertive behavior.
• "I/S/C"s do well with people and tasks, but tend not to be drivers.

Summary

The higher the individual's DISC personality type is, in contrast to what their role as a leader is, the greater the potential for making a mistake. For example, if you are a "C" type personality in the role as a leader that requires a lot of "I" type, you may be too reserved. But if you are a "C" type trying to lead a group of "I"s, that's what they need, but you must adapt your style to be more excited. "I"s prefer someone to take care of the details and paper work. But "I"s also need someone positive and encouraging. You must decide which factors are most essential and become "all things to all people."

DISC Learning Styles

According to Cynthia Tobias' book, *THE WAY THEY LEARN*, there are four basic learning styles: Concrete, Abstract, Sequential, and Random. There are also three ways we remember. She adds, "Learning styles researchers Walter Barbe and Raymond Swassing present three modes of sensory perception (ways of remembering) that we all use in varying degrees." These "modalities" (auditory, visual, and kinesthetic) affect everyone's learning styles.

Every leader should discover their auditory, visual, or kinesthetic / feeling styles in order to help communicate better with their followers and fellow leaders. It is not always their follower's fault when things are misunderstood. It is every leader's responsibility to work with others to know how they learn best.

Leaders should also know and understand how these learning styles respond. Adapting one's presenting style to the learning style of others will often determine the success or failure of a relationship. It is not always the responsibility of the follower to adapt his or her learning style to that of the leader. Followers and leaders must both control their communicating and learning styles in order to have the best results possible.

Understanding how your DISC personalities affect learning styles can help guard your strengths and avoid your weaknesses. Study the insights below to improve your communicating and learning. Always remember, you are the only one who can control yourself to do right.

Do not expect or depend on anyone else to give you the determination to respond appropriately. Learn to control your personality, rather than letting your personality control you. Take command of your feelings and thinking, rather than expecting others to change on your behalf.

Become a more effective Transformational Leader by adapting your leading style to the learning styles of others.

"D" Behavior

Auditory Learner: LISTENS best to challenges and straightforward communication. Wants to hear bottom-line and summarized facts. Does not like to listen to long drawn-out stories. Responds best to serious and hard-hitting points. Pays most attention when lessons are direct and demanding.

Visual Learner: Wants to SEE progress and results. Responds best to action-packed visuals. Learns best when lessons are animated or shown, as opposed to written or spoken. Desires more hands on group learning by example.

Kinesthetic Learner: Wants to FEEL in control of learning. Desires strong emotion-packed, as opposed to sensitive or silly type presentations. Responds best to authority who makes him or her relate personally to the learning.

"I" Behavior

Auditory Learner: LISTENS best to exciting and enthusiastic communication. Desires to hear expressions and word-pictures that make lessons come alive. Needs to hear influencing and impressive learning that communicates optimism. Hears the lesson best through humorous stories.

Visual Learner: Wants to SEE the lesson through drama or role-play. Desires to participate by acting out or visualizing the lesson. Learns best when able to picture him or herself in the lesson. Looks for images that explain the lesson.

Kinesthetic Learner: Wants to FEEL part of the lesson. Desires an emotional tie with the presenter and point of the lesson. Learns best in a group where his or her feelings can be expressed. Needs heartfelt communication.

"S" Behavior

Auditory Learner: LISTENS best to sweet and soft presentations. Does not like strong or fast-paced communication. Responds best to supportive and security-oriented words. Desires to hear lessons in a small group. Wants to hear words that make the lesson kind, nice, and caring.

Visual Learner: Wants to SEE the lesson lived-out through the life of the presenter. Learns best by visualizing the lesson as part of a small group, rather than having to be up front presenting. Desires steady and stable visual environments.

Kinesthetic Learner: Wants to FEEL comfortable and secure as he or she learns. Responds best to status-quo type learning, without surprises or challenges. Desires that everyone is learning harmoniously and together as a family. Needs to feel the lesson in a personal and private way.

"C" Behavior

Auditory Learner: LISTENS best to clear and precise words. Desires to hear lessons that explain why, what, when, and how. Wants to hear competent and accurate communication. Is not as interested in the drama, but in hearing the facts. Learns best with thorough explanation.

Visual Learner: Wants to SEE the lesson, as opposed to just hearing about it. Desires visualization of the facts. Learns best when presented with investigated lessons. Needs to have pictures and charts drawn that explain the lesson.

Kinesthetic Learner: Wants to FEEL the lesson is clear and understandable. Learns best when communicated through rational and emotional means. Desires balance between facts and feelings. Wants to learn through heartfelt, yet intellectual presentations. Needs to feel the lesson is logical.

There is so much we can learn from science and common sense. It is obvious how some people respond to different speakers, while they are not at all interested in others. We have all experienced great interest listening to one type of communicator, while others seem to bore us.

At the same time, we have seen how our friends get really

turned on to the same message that does nothing to us. It is sometimes more than style or subject. It can be the words and phrases speakers use to grab our attention. It is not an art. It is an ability to get into the minds and hearts of those who are listening, whether they realize it or not.

Neurolinguistic Programming

Neurolinguistic Programming (NLP) is the unique way our minds often process what we say and hear. Scientists have discovered that the neurons in our brains are the information highways that pass along everything we see, hear, and feel. When these neurons get disconnected or out of line, our memory is affected. When we have healthy minds and the neurons pass information along freely, we have optimal mental well-being.

We have also found that our brains "wake-up" and become more active when certain words and phrases are processed based on our personalities. Our minds literally light up and show more alertness. The following insights are simple observations of how people verbally share their thoughts, and how people perceive what they hear.

Everyone processes what they experience through their unique senses. There is no normal right or wrong way of processing what we hear. Some leaders can intuitively "read between the lines" of those who are silently hurting, while other leaders are better able to say just the right words at the right time.

The problem is that we tend to lean toward, and be controlled by, our specific NLP. Under pressure and stress we lean toward our strengths, because that is where we are most comfortable and confident. But the overuse of a strength can become an abuse and the best thing about us can become the worst.

By identifying and understanding our NLP from a DISC personality perspective, we can guard our strengths and avoid our weaknesses (uniquenesses) while communicating to others. We can consciously use the most effective words to influence others. We can also be aware of the words others may use that best influence us.

So when you speak to an individual or a group, keep in mind that people listen through their NLP. You will also have the natural tendency to share through your NLP. Therefore, consider the words you use. Adapt your presentation to the person you are trying to communicate with to fit their NLP. Also when speaking to a group of people, be sure to add the words and phrases with which everyone can identify.

For example, when making an appeal to a group you may want to say something like this as you close: "I challenge you to take this risk"; and "People will see and take note of your wisdom"; and "I want to sincerely encourage you to make this decision"; and "Doesn't this decision make sense?" Also keep in mind there is a lot of "junk" associated with human behavior science. Choose what you use carefully.

"D" Types
Listen for, and often use, the following words or phrases:

Words: challenge, power, powerful, big, better, results, bottom-line, win, work, change, strong, stronger, stand, direct, definite, demand, decisiveness, deviance, now.

Phrases: if it doesn't work, let's change it; do something; get-in or get-out; lead, follow, or get out of the way; my way or the highway; bigger and better; I'm results-oriented; I don't like the status-quo; things need to change around here; we need to work harder; let's not be so sensitive; take a stand; stand in the gap; give it to me straight; don't beat around the bush; I demand; I'm determined; I've decided; now is the time; let's not wait any longer.

"I" Types

Listen for, and often use, the following words or phrases:

Words: exciting, enthusiasm, fun, feel, joy, joyful, positive, inspiring, impressive, interesting, fantastic, wow, awesome, wonderful, phenomenal, thrilling, sensational.

Phrases: isn't this exciting or fun?; I'm so excited; let's be enthusiastic; let's all do it together; I really care about you; I feel your pain; something good is going to happen; I feel great; how is this going to effect the crowd?; let's go for it; let me tell you this story; let me illustrate this; you're going to really like this; can you believe this?; watch me, this is sensational; I'm overwhelmed; I'm elated; I sincerely want to help you.

"S" Types

Listen for, and often use, the following words or phrases:

Words: caring, nice, kind, sensitive, sweet, soft, tender, loving, belonging, family, tradition, steady, stable, security, serving, servant, teamwork, unity, calm.

Phrases: I really care about you; let's not hurt anyone; we need to be more sensitive; how will this affect our family?; doesn't anyone care?; I don't like change just for change sake; let's take it slow; I don't like instability or insecurity; I like stable and steady situations; people are more important than things; his or her feelings really matter; how can we help that person?; let's work together; united we can; we're in this together; let me help you; I'm not sure I can do that; I really don't feel comfortable.

"C" Types
Listen for, and often use, the following words or phrases:

Words: think, analyze, reason, evaluate, investigate, comprehend, understand, plan, contingency, process, due-diligence, organize; explain, cautious, careful, conscientious, consider, contemplate, study, research.

Phrases: the intelligent thing to do; it's the reasonable thing to do; I don't understand; please explain; let's think about this; I need time to think; doesn't this make sense?; let's process this; we need a backup plan; let's work our plan and plan our work; we need to work smarter; we need to be more organized; I can't stand disorganization; let's be more careful; let's look further; I don't like quick decisions; I hate sloppy work; figure it out.

Good Advice

Once we recognize how we tend to communicate according to how we are wired, we can become conscientious of the words and phrases we use, and the way others are hearing us. We should then learn how to control our communication to affect others according to the way they are wired.

We should never use this knowledge to intimidate or manipulate people. It will often backfire on us and the results will be worst than what we desired. Wise leaders think first of the needs of others and communicate with the interests of others in mind.

Now let us look at how all this affects our Team Building efforts.

Point #5

Effective Team Building stands on the pillars of personality profiling!

Team Building involves people working as a group, but there has to be a leader of leaders. The "leader" of the team must be able to inspire others through contagious influence and a clear focus on the common cause.

Vision Casting

One of the most important qualities of good leaders is the ability to cast a vision of what needs to be done. The following is how each personality type should cast a vision so that all the other types respond effectively. Leaders *lead*. That means leaders are moving others toward a goal.

"D" types

"D" leaders are the most natural at casting the vision. They are extremely motivated to get others to follow. They are often too pushy and demanding. They do not like indecisive or unresponsive individuals. "D" followers can be difficult. They do not like to be told what to do. The greatest challenge is for "D" leaders to allow others to be involved in the vision casting. They are best at seeing the big picture, but need to be more sensitive while getting others to move forward. "D"s need to slow down and prepare their moves.

"I" types

"I"s tend to be the most enthusiastic while casting their visions. They often envision more than can be accomplished. They need to guard what they dream. The most important situation for an "I" leader to avoid is getting too emotional. "I"s have great verbal skills and use their words as master craftsmen. They should use this strength to influence others without manipulating them to fulfill THE vision. "I"s need to be more cautious and calculating while leading others.

"S" types

"S" leaders cast their vision in subtle ways. They do not get really excited. They often approach their vision with uncertainty and may even apologize for being a little far out. They can act just like "D"s if pushed into a corner, especially if it affects their security. "S" leaders are the most gentle and accommodating. Everyone should learn from "S"s when it comes to staying calm and genuinely trying to make others happy. They should be more aggressive and assertive.

"C" types

"C"s can be the most precision vision casters. They drive non-"C" followers crazy with the fine print. "C" leaders come across as unbending. They need to be more tolerant and understanding. "C" followers, dealing with "C" leaders, can get into heated debates over right or wrong. Of course, "the leader should still be in charge!" When the "C" leader knows the follower is wrong, the leader should share as many logical reasons as possible why the vision will not work.

NOTE: Leaders need to deal with each of their followers according to their specific personalities. For instance, cast your vision to a "D" with respect and the big-picture. Cast your vision to the "I" enthusiastically. Respond to the "S" with slowness and security. And cast your vision to the "C" followers with patience and explanations.

One of the best ways to see the big picture of your group's profile is to combine the members on one graph to see the dynamics of the group's personality.

Combined Graph

Combining two to five people on the same graph can be very enlightening. See how your DISC type relates to another person's or the group's graphs. Parent, Couples, Team Leaders, Supervisors, Business Managers and Owners can now assess their staffs or family as a group by having each person in the group complete his or her profile and then plot their results on the same graphs. See the example that follows.

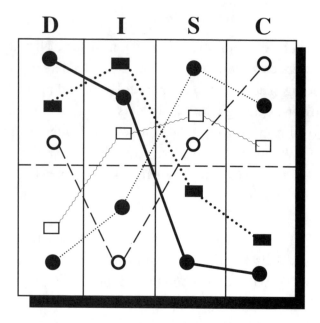

There is also an entire section in some of the online *Uniquely You Profiles* at: www.uniquelyyou.NET that allows you to compare the graphs of different people. Up to five individuals in a family, or on a staff or team can see their group dynamics and develop strategies to improve their effectiveness.

This is also great for a parent or child to glean insights from up to four other family members. Parents can use this feature to identify why certain members of the family conflict with each other.

Couples can also combine their individual graphs to contrast their specific personality types. Dating and engaged couples should especially identify their strengths and "uniqueness."

Each person in a group, family, or relationship must first purchase and complete his or her profile at: *www.uniquelyyou. NET*. Then click on the *photo link* you want to complete.

Once you have logged-in, go to *My Account*, complete the questionnaire, and then click on *Complete a Group Graph*. You may choose two to five person's profiles on Graph 1 "This is Expected of Me" and Graph 2 "This is Me" from a DISC perspective.

The Combined Graphs are one of the best functions and enlightening features of the *Uniquely You Profiles*.

The Ideal Team

The best Team Building involves understanding the personalities and motivations of everyone involved and how to deal with all the differences they bring to the team. Assessing each individual's contribution to the team is vital. I always advise: "Staff to your weaknesses." Wise team building is an essential element for success. We need to be careful that we do not surround ourselves with people just like us.

The former Mayor Rudy Giuliani titled one of the chapters in his book, *Leadership*, "Surround Yourself with Great People." He also wrote, "Looking back, I believe that the skill I developed better than any other was surrounding myself with great people. The strong — especially since so much of what we had to do in the light of the disaster had no precedent. The axiom about good teamwork making each member of a team better really proved true. I can barely describe what it meant to me to know that I could turn something over to someone and know that it would get done, without having to hector or micromanage."

Without this type of thinking and planning, team building can be disastrous. Giuliani also emphasized, "Analyze Strengths And Weaknesses (Including Your Own)." Recognizing our differences and identifying everyone's value to the team is crucial.

Little Red Riding Hood Lesson

Once upon a time, to protect herself from the big bad *wolf*, *Little Red Riding Hood* disguised herself as a *wolf*.

The *wolf*, in order to sneak up on *Little Red Riding Hood*, disguised itself as the *grandmother.*

And the *grandmother*, in order to confuse the *wolf*, disguised herself as *Little Red Riding Hood.*

The *wolf*, disguised as the *grandmother,* was able to get close enough to kill the *grandmother*, who was disguised as *Little Red Riding Hood.*

Realizing that *Little Red Riding Hood* was really the *grandmother*, the *wolf* was confused. The *wolf* disguised as the *grandmother* then took off running through the woods.

Little Red Riding Hood, who was disguised as the *wolf* saw what happened and realized her *grandmother* was actually the *wolf* who began running through the woods.

Little Red Riding Hood, disguised as the *wolf*, took off after the *wolf*, who was disguised as the *grandmother*.

Hunters seeing a *wolf*, who was really *Little Red Riding Hood*, chasing a *grandmother*, who was really the big bad *wolf*, shot and killed *Little Red Riding Hood,* because they thought she was the *wolf*.

The *wolf*, disguised as the *grandmother*, continued running through the woods.

Other wolves, thinking the big bad *wolf* was a *grandmother* lost in the woods, attacked and killed what they thought was a *grandmother*, but who was really a *wolf*. [1]

[1] The author of this book is not aware of the source of the *Little Red Riding Hood* lesson and would like to know so due credit can be given.

When we do not know who we or others actually are, the results can be tragic!

Identifying personality types and why you and others do what you do can be so enlightening. These insights can help solve the mystery of motivation. They are ancient truths for modern times!

An unexamined life is not worth living!
Aristotle

Great leaders turn difficulties into direction. They learn how to identify what motivates their followers by understanding their personality types. They also develop a passion that casts vision and inspires their followers.

Team Building Reflections

You can also contrast two or more individual's personality profiles on a paper instrument using Graphs 1 and 2.

Transpose the results from each person's graphs. To observe the possible differences in the profiles use different color ink pens or various dotted line in contrast to a solid lines. Notice the sample graph.

Once everyone on the team has completed his or her profile, ask the following questions:

Graph 1 Observations:

How many High "D"s are there above the mid-line? (indicates more Determined behavior):

How many High "I"s are there above the mid-line? (indicates more Inspiring behavior):

How many High "S"s are there above the mid-line? (indicates more Stable behavior):

How many High "C"s are there above the mid-line? (indicates more Cautious behavior):

How many High "S"s and "C"s above the mid-line? (indicates more Task-oriented behavior):

How many High "I"s and "S"s above the mid-line? (indicates more People-oriented behavior):

If there are more "D"s and "I"s, than there are "S"s and "C"s, the Team tends to be more Active, than Passive and vice-versa.

If there are more "D"s and "C"s, than there are "I"s and "S"s, the Team tends to be more Task-oriented, than People-oriented and vise-versa.

Who are the High "D"s on the Team?

Who are the High "I"s on the Team?

Who are the High "S"s on the Team?

Who are the High "C"s on the Team?

Is the Team more Active or Passive?

Is the Team more Task or People-oriented?

What is the Team's average personality profile in Graph 1?
(If you use a paper instrument, to determine the Team's average, add everyone's DISC totals and divide by the number of people in the group. If you have everyone in the group do an online profile, the computer will do this for you.)

Graph 2 Observations:

How many High "D"s are there above the mid-line? (indicates more Determined behavior):

How many High "I"s are there above the mid-line? (indicates more Inspiring behavior):

How many High "S"s are there above the mid-line? (indicates more Stable behavior):

How many High "C"s are there above the mid-line? (indicates more Cautious behavior):

How many High "S"s and "C"s above the mid-line? (indicates more Passive behavior):

How many High "I"s and "S"s above the mid-line? (indicates more People-oriented behavior):

If there are more "D"s and "I"s, than there are "S"s and "C"s, the Team tends to be more Active, than Passive and vice-versa.

If there are more "D"s and "C"s, than there are "I"s and "S"s, the Team tends to be more Task-oriented, than People-oriented and vice-versa.

Who are the High "D"s on the Team?

Who are the High "I"s on the Team?

Who are the High "S"s on the Team?

Who are the High "C"s on the Team?

Is the Team more Active or Passive?

Is the Team more Task or People-oriented?

What is the Team's average personality profile in Graph 2?
(If you use a paper instrument, to determine the Team's average, add everyone's DISC totals and divide by the number of people in the group. If you have everyone in the group do an online profile, the computer will do this for you.)

Team Building Action Plan

Observing the two *TEAM BUILDING REFLECTIONS* Graphs and the notes pages, how would you describe each Team member and the Team as a whole?

Example:

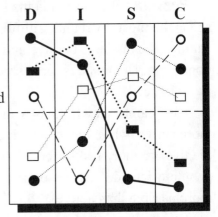

Person #1 (●) tends to be most demanding and decisive. He or she also has good verbal skills. He or she is more concerned about getting the job done, as opposed to security and status quo. He or she does not like details or having to be cautious about everything.

Person #2 (■) is also dominant, but more verbal than the others. He or she is extremely positive and enthusiastic. Concerned about making good impressions, he or she prefers the crowd, as opposed to individuals. He or she is also not interested in doing the little, behind the scenes, things.

Person #3 (○) is more demanding than not, but very particular about getting the job done correctly. He or she is not interested in speaking to groups, but rather working with individuals. He or she is more task-oriented, plus prefers a steady and stable environment.

Person #4 (☐) is not dominant. He or she loves people and is able to relate to groups, as well as individuals. Though interested in correctness, he or she is not a "perfectionist", but may demonstrate more "concern" for doing things right. He or she is more people-oriented.

Person #5 (●– –) is the least assertive and decisive. He or she is the most loyal and faithful. Concerned about security and stability, he or she is passive and particular about getting things done right. He or she is more shy, but makes a faithful friend to those in need.

The Team, as a whole, is well-balanced. Two of the five are more active, while two of the five are more passive. Two of the five are more task-oriented, while two of the five are more people-oriented. One person is both active and passive, but is more passive than active.

The predominant trait of the Team is slightly more active than passive with 12 of the 20 plotting points above the mid-line. This group is also more verbal and may compete for attention. They can draw on each other's strengths, while avoiding their individual weaknesses to benefit the Team.

This Team may need to improve with a little more stable and cautious behavior. They may also need to be more passive and reserved. Listening and showing more concern for others will improve their effectiveness.

Be positive, but honest with your comments. These notes will be shared with everyone. The purpose is not to expose or hurt anyone, but to improve our understanding and effectiveness of one another.

Person #1's Name and type:

Person #2's Name and type:

Person #3's Name and type:

Person #4's Name and type:

Person #5's Name and type:

How do you see the Team as whole?

What do you think the Team needs to improve?

Once you identify and understand your team's dynamic design, you can begin focusing on the more specific needs of each of the individuals you work with and relate to.

Most challenges for a team can be avoided in the hiring process. Finding the right people for the right job is vital. Personality profiling can solve most problems even before you complete your team.

Knowing ahead of time the type of personality you are looking for can be time-saving and beneficial. Profiling applicants can also be very enlightening. You do not want to only look for one type of personality. First look for integrity and experience. Sometimes the right person is someone who has learned to control his or her personality and no matter what the results of his or her personality assessment.

Learning how to also ask the right questions in the interview process can be very useful. The following will help you build a team that will be most effective.

Job / Profile Indicator

To contrast a prospective employee to a role you are trying to fill, compare the personality of the person you would like to find for that specific job. Transpose the graphs (employee and employer must each complete a *Uniquely You Questionnaire*).

The employer should do the *UYQ* with the specific job needs (role) in mind. In other words, the employer should choose the words in the *UYQ* he or she would prefer the applicant choosing.

To observe the possible differences in the profiles use two different color ink pens, or a pen and pencil, or a dotted line in contrast to a solid line.

You can also profile the specific role of all prospective employees online by going to: *www.uniquelyyou.NET*, then click on *Professionals / Leaders* link. Be sure to complete the online questionnaire as if you were the person you were looking for to fill the specific role you need. Choose the adjectives you want the new employee to be, not the adjectives that describe you. Notice the sample graph below.

The person with the solid line has a "D/I" personality, while the person with a dotted line has a "S/C" personality. One type is not better than the other. Both personalities have their strengths and "uniquenesses." To improve your interviewing, notice the differences.

Prospective employees and their jobs often conflict because of prospects' personalities and job demands. If the solid

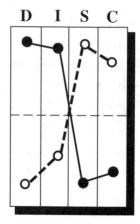

line is that of the prospect, this person wants to dominate — to be in charge. But the employer knows total freedom is not possible. The employer may naturally resist hiring this person.

But the "D/I" prospect may be exactly what this job needs. The "D/I" may want to do his or her own thing, while the "S/C" employer may want to make sure the person is careful. The "D/I" prospect wants be more aggressive, while the "S/C" employer may want the prospect to be more reserved.

The "S/C" employer needs to be more assertive in order to control the "D/I" employee. The "S/C" employer also needs to be aware of the "D/I" prospect's need for opportunity to "run with the ball." This prospect is a self-starter, but will need to work under authority.

On the other hand, "D/I" employers must control themselves first if they want to control their employees. "S/C" employees must always remember certain personalities are control-oriented and need to be instantly obeyed. Employees will gain more freedom and responsibility when they learn to obey, rather than resist strong "D" type employers.

Notice all "D," "I," "S," and "C" differences in the graphs the employer completed in respect to the job and the graphs of the potential employee. Do not concentrate on the predominantly high letter. Evaluate each letter with the specific job description in mind.

Job Intensity Factors

Placing the right person in the right job obviously makes a difference. Hiring the right personality for a specific job is imperative. The following are examples and explanations of how to interview and hire people according to their personalities, as well as abilities and experiences.

Stress occurs in every job. The level of pressure can be directly related to the employee's personality in relation to his or her job demands. In other words, aggressive sales presentation will cause more stress to the passive and reserved type personality. "D" and "I" type personalities are more suited to sales positions.

At the same time, "S" salespeople can be successful as they control their natural reluctance and discipline themselves to be more outgoing. Their sales style will be "steady, stable and sensitive," emphasizing service and security (trust) as they sell.

Interviewing Insights

The following 21 Behavioral Blends have specific questions designed for you to ask in an interview situation. Be sure to first identify the interviewee's personality profile by administering the questionnaire. Once he or she has completed the UYQ, study the two graphs, then find the most similar configurations. The graphs may not be exactly alike. Look for the configurations that are most similar to both graphs.

Ask the questions designated to each graph. Take notes for future reference. Do not use this assessment to influence whether you will hire or fire anyone. You may also want to ask other questions listed for similar profiles relating to the person's highest plotting point.

For example, if the person is a high "D/I" - "Driving Influencer" blend, you may also want to ask some of the questions that relate to the "Inspirational Influencer" or "Driving Competent Type" blends. Do not make any conclusions or references to this instrument as you perceive the person's traits. Speak in generalities. Ask the person if what you are saying is accurate. Listen closely to the person's answers, plus evaluate his or her experience and ability.

Check all the references.

Look for maturity and experience in learning how to control personality differences. There is no "best" personality for any job. The qualities that may suit one person better than another, over-used, may be the very reason for disqualification.

Be sure to focus on each letter, whether high, low or mid, and design your own questions relating to specific job needs. You should study this entire section to better understand personality types. Training is also available for those who want to become "Certified Human Behavior Consultants" and learn how to conduct Human Resources training and / or individual coaching for individuals or organizations who want to improve their effectiveness.

Once you identify the personality type of a prospective employee or team member, you should interview him or her with the following questions.

PERSONAL INSIGHTS / INTERVIEWING QUESTIONS

D: DETERMINED DOERS
• How well do you work under authority? Explain.
• How do the feelings of others affect your decision-making?
• Do you relate well to people and why or why not?
• How do you resolve conflicts with people?
• How do you motivate people to be productive?
• What are your long-range plans?
• What do you think about quality versus quantity?
• How do you guard against dominating people?

D/I: DRIVING INSPIRER TYPES

• How do you motivate people?
• What do you think about passive behavior?
• How would you handle unenthusiastic people?
• How would you follow a leader less able than you?
• How important is thorough research and preparation?
• How do you deal with being or not being patient?
• How do you follow the chain-of-command?
• When would you delegate a task for which you are responsible?

D/C: DRIVING COMPETENT TYPES

• How well do you work with people?
• How important are friends to you?
• How are you trying to improve your people skills?
• Where do you draw the line between getting the job done and people's feelings?
• How do you relax?
• How would you handle speaking to a large group about your work?
• What do you think about team participation and how would you develop it?

I: INSPIRATIONAL INFLUENCERS

• How punctual are you and how do you guard against poor time management?
• How do you feel about paperwork and completing written reports?
• How do you deal with rejection?
• How much do you research and prepare for beginning a project?
• How do you avoid always winging it?
• How good are your listening skills?

• What would you do if someone got credit for something you did?

I/D: INSPIRATIONAL DOERS

• How would you respond to someone who makes you look bad?
• How do you defend and guard against exaggeration?
• How do you deal with failure in yourself and others?
• How do you relax and handle stress?
• How would you respond if you were overlooked for a promotion?
• How would you handle an unmotivated peer?
• How would you like to be recognized?

I/S: INSPIRATIONAL SPECIALISTS

• How well do you manage your time?
• How would you deal with completing a task and not offending others who demand your time?
• How would you tell people you need to finish your work if they want to talk to you?
• How would you handle having to fire or lay off a good friend or faithful employee?
• Where does your duty to the company end and your loyalty to family begin?
• How would you handle an overbearing supervisor or an intolerable manager?

I/C: INSPIRATIONAL COMPETENT TYPES

• How well do you take criticism?
• How would you handle a jealous co-worker?
• What motivates you to work hard when alone?
• If you weren't given the time or resources to do a job right, what would you do?
• How loyal do you think you will be to the company?

- What would you do if you saw a friend doing something wrong at work?
- How do you deal with mood swings?
- How do you guard yourself against a desire to correct others?

S: STEADY SPECIALISTS
- How do you deal with conflicts?
- Could you fire someone—especially a close friend?
- How would you handle an irate customer or fellow employee?
- How excited can you get about working here?
- What would you do if you saw something that wasn't right?
- How aggressive can you be to get the job done?
- What would the last straw be to make you quit?

S/I: STEADY INFLUENCERS
- What time management skills do you practice?
- Have you ever confronted a good friend about a problem and how did you do it?
- When is compromise unacceptable?
- How do you handle forceful people?
- How do you deal with those who criticize you?
- How much do you prepare for a lecture or presentation?
- How self-motivated are you?
- What do you know about assertiveness training?

S/D: STEADY DOERS
- How good are you at speaking to large groups?
- How would you inspire people to do their jobs?
- Where do you draw the line between protecting friendship and getting the job done?
- How would you ignite a dull environment?

- Give me an example of how you would go about planning a special project.
- How far would you go in your research of a specific solution?
- When is anger appropriate?

S/C: STEADY COMPETENT TYPES

- Would you be willing to take a public speaking course?
- How do you guard yourself against moodiness?
- How would you handle making a presentation to a large group?
- What would you do if you didn't have enough time to do a job right?
- What excites you most about your jobs?
- How would you handle an over-zealous person?
- How would you correct a sensitive co-worker?

C: CAUTIOUS COMPETENT TYPES

- What do you think about people who do their work half-way? How do you deal with them?
- How well do you handle deadlines?
- Do you carry grudges and how do you resolve conflicts with people who hurt you?
- How well can you work under an incompetent supervisor?
- How are you friendly to people you don't know?
- How would you deal with a fellow employee who has a problem with another employee?

C/S: COMPETENT SPECIALISTS

- When have you ever been too "picky" about a task?
- How do you handle those who want you to finish a job half-way?
- How do you deal with overly optimistic people?
- How do you guard against depression and pessimism?

• How do you get others to have good attitudes?
• How do you decide when to take risks?
• How can you improve your people skills?

I/C/S (or any combination of I, S, and C):
INSPIRING COMPETENT SPECIALISTS

• How are you challenged to do unappealing jobs?
• When and how would you confront a friend and co-worker who is not doing his or her job right?
• What would you do if a supervisor told you to do something that was absolutely wrong?
• How aggressive would you be about getting a job done on time?
• How do you deal with a co-worker who doesn't like you?

C/S/D (or any combination of D, S, and C):
COMPETENT STEADY DOERS

• How would you describe your people skills?
• Why and how important is friendliness?
• How would you handle those who oppose your ideas and decisions?
• How well do you speak to large crowds?
• How would you guard against doing everything yourself, rather than delegating to others?
• Are you more serious or relaxed and why, when you speak to groups.
• How would you get a group to follow your ideas?

I/D/S (or any combination of D, I, and S):
INSPIRING DRIVING SUBMISSIVE

• How do you deal with excessive paper work?
• How do you guard against overlooking the little details?

- When and why is too much optimism dangerous?
- How would you relate to someone who is extremely pessimistic or detailed-oriented?
- How would you confront a good friend and co-worker who is out of line?
- When and why is there a need for balance between getting the job done and getting it done right?

D/I/C (or any combination of D, I, and C): DOMINANT INSPIRING CAUTIOUS

- How important is loyalty and why?
- How do you relax when the pressure is on?
- When and why are the needs of an individual more important than those of the group or project?
- How do you guard against impatience with those who are slow or incompetent?
- How long do you expect to continue at this job?
- How do you deal with obeying a supervisor who tells you do something you don't agree with?

STRAIGHT MID-LINE

- How do you guard against being indecisive?
- What do you think your greatest strengths are?
- What do you think your greatest weaknesses are?
- How do you deal with people who seem to exaggerate their feelings or ideas?
- How do you respond when you need to be more enthusiastic?
- How would you describe your aggressiveness?
- How do you deal with the need to be more or less cautious at times?

ABOVE MID-LINE
- How do you deal with your drive to overachieve?
- How do you relax?
- How do you respond to people who seem to be weak in certain areas?

BELOW MID-LINE
- What do you think about yourself?
- How do you deal with depression?
- How do you respond to overly optimistic people?
- How do you deal with discouragement?

Our challenging differences often divide or unite us. We tend to gravitate toward those who are opposite of us. But once we are in a working or more intimate relationship, we tend to resist those who are different from us. We should always remember this dynamic from Human Behavior Science and guard these natural tendencies.

We should learn to appreciate all those around us and recognize everyone's contribution to our lives. Each member of a team or family is vital and important. Treat them accordingly and begin enjoying your relationships, rather than just enduring them.

Point #6

Challenging differences often divide or unite us!
(How to handle conflicts)

The tie that binds can also become the cord that strangles or hangs us. There is nothing more precious than dear relationships and there is nothing that hurts more than strained friendships. At home and work, our personality differences often make or break us.

Challenging Differences

Opposite personalities are often attracted to each other to "complete" themselves or they clash like fire and gas. We are often attracted to people who have opposite personalities to us because they fill our lives with those things we tend to need. There are probably obvious differences between you and your friends and team members.

How different is your personality to your team members' and closest friends'? Your strengths are their weaknesses and vice-versa. Begin thinking about the so-called "weaknesses" of others as "uniqueness."

It is natural for us to gravitate toward roles that fit our personalities. We may find ourselves struggling in roles where our temperaments are tested. Our comfort zones are bordered by the parameters of our personalities. In other words, life is easier when our personalities are not stretched beyond their limits.

My wife and I are good examples of active and passive types. I am more active and she is more passive. Opposites do attract and they also can "attack," oops, I mean, attract and "attach." We are definitely opposite personalities, but she is the best thing that ever happened to me!

I really believe she was attracted to me to complete me. Sometimes, I think, "to finish me off!" She has helped to temper and soften my aggressiveness and boldness, while I have helped her to improve her assertiveness and to not be so shy or quiet.

Do opposites really attract or not?

I noticed a CNN article recently stating that human behavior scientists have concluded that opposites do attract. As I read closely, I saw where the scientists had only compared couples with similar values, faiths, and preferences. They wrote nothing about differences in personalities and how opposite personalities tended to attract each other.

Couples with similar values, religions, and preferences *do* attract, but they also tend to have opposite personalities according to my research.

Opposites do seem to attract each other. Somehow we are attracted to people who have strengths that are our weaknesses. "C"s will meet an exciting, positive, upbeat type person, like an "I". "C"s will wish they were more like him or her, while the "I" is impressed with the "C"s' logical thinking and organized behavior.

"D"s are often attracted to "C"s because of "C"s cautious and calculating demeanor, while "C"s are impressed with "D"s' risk-taking, driving, decisive and dreaming behavior. "I"s are also attracted to "S"s because of their quiet, sweet, soft demeanor; while "S"s admire "I"s' ability to influence and impress others.

What happens when opposites attract can be explained by the dynamics of differences. Our differences draw us together. Ironically, those same differences can drive us apart. The characteristics of the person with whom we felt a bond often become the very traits we end up resenting.

While opposites often attract, we must keep in mind that most people are blends or composites of DISC. Few people are predominate "D"s, "I"s, "S"s, or "C"s. Most people are a combination of several of types.

Contrasting Personalities

There are "D/I" behavior types, who are active in their tasks and people skills. There are "S/C" types, who are passive, while both people and task-oriented. "D/C"s are pure task-oriented types, while being active and passive. "I/S"s on the other hand, are basically people-oriented while active and passive.

The "I/C" is both active and passive while people and task-oriented at the same time. The same goes for the "D/S." But while the "I/C" loves to inspire and correct, the "D/S" enjoys dominating and serving others. The "D/S" type may sound like a contradiction in terms, but this unique and often confusing behavior is normal.

The most obvious conflicts occur when a pure "D/C" task-oriented individual is attracted to a pure "I/S" people-oriented person. These people were probably initially impressed with the other's strengths, which were their own weaknesses. The "D/C" lacks people skills while the "I/S" needs to become more task-oriented and organized.

The exciting news is each needs the other, but difficulty comes when one stops looking at the other's strengths and starts focusing instead on the other's weaknesses. The "D/C" focuses on logical thinking and being industrious, while the "I/S" desires to build relationships and deepen communication. You can see how these two blends of behavior can clash.

"D/I" Relating To "S/C"
- "D/I"s are outgoing, while "S/C"s are passive and reserved.
- "D/I"s are more positive than "S/C"s.
- Both should learn from each other.
- Be committed!

"I/S" Relating To "D/C"
- "I/S"s are people, while "D/C"s are task-oriented.
- "I/S"s are more high-touch than "D/C"s.
- "D/C"s are more high-tech than "I/S"s.
- Both should learn from each other.
- Be committed!

"D" Relating To "I/S/C"
- "D"s are more dominant and demanding.
- "I/S/C"s resist aggression, but respect it.
- "I/S/C"s prefer friendly, secure, and cautious relationships.
- Both should learn from each other.
- Be committed!

Once you grasp the way you can contrast personality types, you will begin to view relationships with a keener sense of understanding. There are no bad contrasts. It is how each person in a relationship or group responds to the other person or persons that really matters.

The following are more examples of possible contrasts. Look for the relationship or group dynamics that fit your situation and see what you can learn. Then study all of the contrasts to get a handle of how all personality types relate to each other.

Intensity Insights

Do not make the mistake of thinking two personalities cannot work well together. In fact, it is sometimes better to have two different personality types working together, so one type will compensate for the other. Remember, we all have blind spots.

Two similar personalities can also work well together, as long as they both respect and trust each other. The purpose of understanding the intensity caused by contrasting personality types is to predict behavior and respond better. Always keep in mind, no personality is better than another. We must learn to understand why people do what they do. We should strive to respond in more mature and wiser ways.

"D" / "D"

Work Index: Two "D"s can work well together as long as one recognizes the other is the "boss." "D" #1 may be the boss, but "D" # 2 must respect and trust him. They must also learn to give-and-take. "D" # 2 may be a little more dominant, but "D" # 1 is also very dominant. "D" team members will be more driving.

Practical Application
• Take turns making major decisions.
• Choose who will decide in specific areas.
• Don't give ultimatums.
• Don't force issues.
• Slow down in making decisions.
• Control yourself, rather than trying to control the other person.
• Learn to relax and control stress.

"D" / "I"

Work Index: "D"s and "I"s working together are very active. The "D" wants to control, while the "I" wants to impress. The "I" wants to talk, while the "D" works. The "D" tends to dominate, while the "I" desires to communicate. The "I" feels as though the "D" does not care, while the "D" thinks the "I" is too sensitive. "D"s are too serious, while "I"s are too impulsive.

Practical Application
• Determine to communicate on the basis of the other person's needs.
• "D"s need to show they really care.
• "I"s need to give "D"s a chance to talk.
• "D"s should praise "I"s more.

- "I"s should be more industrious—workers.
- Don't intimidate or manipulate.

"D" / "S"

Work Index: "D"s and "S"s working together are like masters and slaves. "D"s tell "S"s what to do. "D"s need to appreciate "S"s for their hard work. "D"s definitely dominate "S"s, but should never take them for granted. "S"s feel secure with "D"s as long as "D"s show controlled and stable behavior. "S"s should be assertive — "D"s more compromising.

Practical Application
- "D"s should direct, not dominate "S"s — submit yourself one to the other.
- Agree that when the "D" is out of control, the "S" has the right to say so, without fear.
- "S"s need to strongly appeal to "D"s when their behavior is unacceptable.
- "S"s should show more determination.

"D" / "C"

Work Index: "D" and "C" working together conflict over dreams and details. The "D" wants to get the job done, while the "C" wants to get it done right. "D"s are optimistic, while "C"s are more pessimistic ("realistic"). "D"s need to be more careful, while "C"s need to be more positive. "D" and "C" team members are task- rather than people-oriented.

Practical Application
- Be more understanding of other's perspective — don't criticize their personality.

- Allow others to feel the way they feel.
- "D"s ought to listen more to "C"s.
- "C"s should avoid always being negative.
- Give "C"s chance to think about decision.
- "C"s should take more risks; "D"s should be more careful.

"I" / "I"

Work Index: Two "I"s working together will talk more than work. They compete for praise and approval. They tend to be overly optimistic and enthusiastic. Two "I"s will communicate well, if one does not try to out-talk the other. Each wants lots of attention. Both tend to be emotional. Communication goes two ways—talking and listening. "I" team members are the most expressive.

Practical Application
- Take turns talking.
- Ask the other to repeat back what he or she heard. "I"s don't listen well.
- Record what you agreed upon so there will be no misunderstandings
- Praise each other more than seeking to be praised.

"I" / "S"

Work Index: "I"s and "S"s do not tend to be industrious. They like to "care and share." "I"s are great at PR, while "S"s like customer service. "I"s and "S" relate well together. "I"s are the talkers, while "S"s are the listeners. "I"s want "S"s to tell them how they feel, but "S"s can not seem to get a word in. "I"s love crowds; "S"s prefer small groups. "I" and "S" team members are people-oriented.

Practical Application

- When an "I" asks an "S" a question, the "I" should wait for the "S" to answer.
- "S"s should not let "I"s always interrupt and control every conversation.
- "S"s should ask "I"s to repeat what "S"s say. "I"s tend to think of what they want to say, rather than listen closely.

"I" / "C"

Work Index: "I"s and "C"s make good associates, when the "I"s do the selling and "C"s do paper work. "I"s dislike "C"s pessimism, while "C"s distrust "I"s facts. "I"s and "C"s can conflict, due to their differences. "I"s are more active, while "C"s passive. "I"s are feeling-oriented, while "C"s are task-oriented. They are definitely opposite, but can complement each other.

Practical Application

- "I"s need to trust "C"s' concerns.
- "C"s ought to be more optimistic about "I's' interests.
- "I"s should do their "homework" before trying to convince "C"s about an idea.
- "C"s need to express themselves, instead of internally criticizing "I"s.

"S" / "S"

Work Index: Two "S"s work best together. They do not compete or criticize each other. They are loyal and sensitive to the other. They make great associates. "S"s are the most tolerant and forgiving types; therefore, they make the nicest team members. They tend not to be assertive and will struggle with decision-making. They add stability and sensitivity to the team.

Practical Application
• "S"s should force themselves to express their feelings.
• Two "S"s can miss great opportunities, because neither one wants to take risks.
• Try not to depend on the other for major decisions.
• Be more enthusiastic and outgoing.

"S" / "C"

Work Index: "S"s and "C"s working together will be passive and methodical. Precision and propriety come before performance. "S"s want "C"s to be more friendly. "C"s can be too picky, but "S"s will be most forgiving. "S"s desire more kindness, while "C"s more perfection. They are both more quiet and private. They can work well together with little need for conversation.

Practical Application
• "S"s need to be more demanding with "C"s.
• Work together on projects.
• "C"s should not criticize "S"s' disinterest.
• Be more intimate and aggressive.
• Don't wait on others to express themselves.
• Be more optimistic and positive about your problems.

"C" / "C"

Work Index: Two "C"s working together can be challenging. Both have high standards on how to do things. "C"s tend to think their way is best. Two "C"s will conflict over "right and wrong." They can be cold and caustic. "C"s tend to be picky-perfectionistic and demanding of competence. They make great team members when at peace and when they respect each other.

Practical Application
• Be more complimentary of each other.
• Don't criticize each other's work.
• Don't keep your feelings in.
• Be more expressive and positive.
• Think twice before saying what you think.
• Compromise in your way of doing things.
• Be more outgoing and people-oriented.

Once you understand the different Intensity Insights, you can focus better on how to avoid and resolve conflicts.

How To Handle Conflicts

Often, the greatest hindrances to healthy relationships are personality conflicts. Positive individuals, desiring to build good relationships, are often discouraged because of misunderstandings and clashes with others.

This section is designed to help you discover why people do what they do under pressure and why you may conflict with others. Life's success principles on how to handle clashes are clear. The problem is many people are not aware of their "sensitive spots." Everyone needs to learn more about avoiding and resolving conflicts.

Every personality has its "hot button." Everyone can act like a "D" when pushed too far. The following are tendencies of personalities as they relate under pressure. Review the following pages with your Behavioral Blends in mind.

Read each section to see how you may respond as a specific personality type. Also consider how you may respond differently because of your "hot and cold buttons."

To improve your effectiveness, control your personality and never use it as an excuse for poor behavior! Remember...

*Most problems today are not technical - they are relational —
personality conflicts and clashes with others.*

"D" Behavior

Under Pressure: becomes dictatorial, domineering, demanding, angry, intense, forceful, direct, bossy.

Sources of Irritation: weakness, indecisiveness, laziness, lack of discipline, plan, purpose, direction, authority, control, challenge.

Needs To: back off, seek peace, relax, think before reacting, control self, be: patient, loving, friendly, loyal, kind, sensitive.

"I" Behavior

Under Pressure: becomes hyper, overly optimistic, immature, emotional, irrational, silly, wordy, selfish.

Sources of Irritation: disinterest, slowness, pessimism, details, time restraints, antagonism, doubt, structure, lack of enthusiasm, team participation.

Needs To: listen, count the cost, control emotions, be: humble, strong, disciplined, punctual, careful with words, conscientious.

"S" Behavior

Under Pressure: becomes subservient, insecure, fearful, weak-willed, withdrawn, sympathizer, sucker.

Sources of Irritation: pushiness, instability, inflexibility, anger, disloyalty, insensitivity, pride, discrimination, unfairness.

Needs To: be:strong, courageous, challenging, aggressive, assertive, confrontational, enthusiastic, outgoing, expressive, cautious, bold.

"C" Behavior

Under Pressure: becomes moody, critical, contemplative, negative, worrisome.

Sources of Irritation: incompetence, disorganization, foolishness, dishonesty, inaccuracy, wastefulness, inconsistency, blind faith, false impressions.

Needs To : loosen up, communicate, be: joyful, positive, tolerant, compromising, open, trusting, enthusiastic.

Challenging differences often divide or unite us!

Natural Responses To Conflict

"D"s - Want To Attack
"I"s - Want To Expose Others
"S"s - Want To Support or Submit
"C"s - Want To Criticize

Recommended Wise Responses

"D"s - Restore With Love
"I"s - Make Others Look Good
"S"s - Care Enough To Confront
"C"s - Examine Own Self First

Understanding why people do what they do and how to avoid conflicts, is not enough to avoid and resolve conflicts. You must have a strategic plan. Every organization needs a published and "practiced" policy. Employees and management need to both follow set procedures in order to build harmony and unity.

The following are suggestions to follow for building a solid foundation for successful team building.

Resolution Management Commitment

Avoiding and resolving conflicts are essential when managing people. It is the "people-problems" that cause the greatest hindrance to greater productivity and profits. The following commitment is a simple guide to share with each Team Member.

Promise
As a commitment to Resolution Management, I promise to follow the Principle of Priorities. That is, my priorities are to avoid and resolve conflict, while building harmony and effectiveness in my organization. I will attempt to always go first and alone to the offending person.

First Step
I will not first share the offense with another person. I am committed to restoring our relationship, rather than exposing the person's possible wrong. I recognize most of our problems with people are often personality clashes and I will try to understand their actions based upon their perspective.

Second Step
If going to the person "first alone" does not resolve our differences, I promise to seek a neutral and mature individual who will listen to each of our perspectives of the problem. This person will hopefully be able to shed light on one or both of our blind spots or needs to change in order to resolve the conflict.

I recognize that the "mediator" may reveal or say things I will not like, but believe their interest is to resolve the conflict, rather than take sides. (The "mediator" must be an individual with deep wisdom and highly respected by all those involved.)

Warning

I will not seek to find others who have also been offended, nor share with potential "mediator" my concerns prior to the meeting with my "offending person." The purpose of having a "mediator" is not to validate my hurt, but rather to open my heart and mind to the possible needs I may have regarding my relationship with others.

I realize my friends may naturally listen to my concerns, but also take up my offense. I will, therefore, not cause them to become a party to a possible division and disharmony because of our friendship. Whenever I feel an urge to share the offense with my friends, I will seek to be mature about my hurt.

Confronting Leaders

I believe in following the Chain of Command, other than in grave matters of misconduct or irrefutable illegal activity, I will earnestly follow my leaders. I will not allow anyone to criticize them without following Principle of Priorities and without the specific person present.

If I have a problem with my leaders, I will go "first alone" to them. I will not share with anyone my concern. I will listen and try to understand their perspective of the problem. If I am not satisfied with their explanation and continue to have animosity, I will ask their permission to find a "mediator" who will listen to our conflict.

If the "mediator" finds I have misunderstood the situation and should continue no further, I will trust his or her judgment. If the "mediator" agrees with my concern and finds the leader wrong, but the leader refuses to hear the "mediator," we will then find a group of two or three other "mediators" who will hear the matter and determine what is best to resolve this conflict.

Serious Step

If I continue to find fault with a leader and cannot relate or work in "harmony," I will seek to find another place of employment, rather than cause any conflict and disharmony. I am committed to resolving my conflicts even if it means separating myself from the source of my irritations.

Ultimate Goal

I commit myself to be professional rather than "personal" when it comes to solving my problems with others. I want the best way to resolve my conflicts and will do "right," regardless of my normal and natural feelings. My ultimate goal is to effectively lead by relating best to others.

Establishing Preventive Measures

Perhaps resolving problems between employees could be avoided if organizations first profiled each prospective employee in the hiring process. Identifying an applicant's personality type helps interview him or her with the best probing questions. By discovering how balanced and flexible the person is, you can screen out most problem people and hire more wisely.

Point #7

Building your business is easier when you understand personality types.

Some people think, "Team and Business Building is an art!" Actually, it's not an art at all. It is really a science. It is observable and predictable. Once you identify the elements of wise team and business building, you can duplicate your success.

There are definite insights you can learn and do in order to grow your business toward ultimate success. First, be sure to run your business in a way where it does not end up running you. Focus on the priorities and do not sweat the small things.

Two of the most important disciplines in growing your business are selling and servicing the public. Most people hate selling, but learning how to sell more effectively can make the difference between working for someone else all your life or owning your own business and having others do your selling for you.

We must learn how to sell ourselves, as well as our services. Growing your business also involves being task and people smart. It is all part of being personality wise.

Sales Insights

Most everyone responds to life's challenges and choices according to their personalities. Therefore, businesses that sell and service the public must be personality wise. For example, High "D" customers should not be engaged in small talk. They want sales people who get-to-the-point — the "bottom line." They prefer sales people who are not going to waste their pressing time.

On the other hand, High "S" customers feel more comfortable with sales people more systematic, slower and steady in their approaches. "S"s do not like fast talking, quick paced presentations.

Selling Styles

The following will help you see each personality type's selling style. People tend to sell according to their personalties, rather than adapt to the other person's type.

"D" types: "D"s are take control and be in charge types. They do not like people telling them what to do. "D" sales people can be too pushy and forceful. They need to control their direct and demanding approach to selling. They make great sales people when they learn to slow down, be gentle and not so demanding of others.

"I" types: "I"s are inspiring and enthusiastic. They love to sell and influence others. Naturally great presenters, they tend to talk too much. "I" sales people need to listen more and not be so sensi-

tive to rejection. They are the most impressive and positive sales people. "I"s love crowds, but need also be interested in individuals.

"S" types: "S"s are the sweet, steady and stable sales people. They seldom push or demand anything. They are friendly and loyal, but tend to be too nice. They need to be more aggressive and assertive. Overly sensitive to how people feel, "S"s need to be more optimistic. They hate to take risks. They often miss great opportunities because of their caution. Reliable and relaxed, they are more shy.

"C" types: "C"s are competent and compliant. They go by the book and want to do everything just right. They are thorough and detailed-oriented, but tend to be too informative. "C"s need to be more positive and enthusiastic. They answer questions people are not asking. When optimistic, "C"s are extremely influential. They should not concentrate on problems, but rather focus on the potentials.

Buying Styles

Customers also purchase according to their personalities. The following are the purchasing styles of each personality type.

"D" types: "D"s want the absolute best deal. They like to beat the system — make the final decision. They purchase with power and authority in mind. They wonder, "Will this product make me more respected or stronger?" "D" customers need choices, rather than "get-in or get-out" ultimatums.

"I" types: "I"s purchase with their hearts. They tend to be impulsive buyers. They want products that will make them look good. "I" customers talk a lot. They make great first impressions. Their high egos and ability to persuade often turns them into the sales person in order to get a better deal. Sometimes you do not know who is selling to whom.

"S" types: "S" customers do not make quick decisions. They like sales people who are understanding and gentle. They want to establish a relationship with a company that will be around a long time. "S"s are concerned about service and stability. When it comes to sensible and slow judgment, "S" customers feel right at home. They like familiar and low-key environments.

"C" types: "C"s are "Consumer Report" type customers. They research and prepare each purchase. They also love "double coupon" redemption days. "C"s are quality buyers. They do not like cheap products. Picky and precise, they purchase through their minds, rather than hearts. "C"s seldom ever buy anything quickly. They often want time to think about their decisions.

Servicing Styles

Service personnel and customers also respond to needs according to their personalities. The following is how each personality predictably responds to a need for service.

"D" types: "D" customers want their problems solved immediately. They do not like indecisive or unresponsive individuals. "D" service personnel can be difficult. They do not like customers who tell them what to do. The greatest challenge is for a "D" service personnel to allow "D" customers to feel as though they are in charge. At the same time, companies can only give so much. But "D" customers should never be antagonized or threatened. You can not win over an angry "D" customer.

"I" types: "I"s tend to be the most excitable customers. They exaggerate their problems and often claim the ridiculous. "I" service personnel can also promise more than the company can provide. They need to guard what they say. The most important situation for an "I" employee to avoid is getting emotionally involved. "I"s have great verbal skills and use their words as master craftsmen. They should use this strength to solve people-problems, rather than create more problems.

"S" types: "S" customers hate confronting problems. They often apologize for causing trouble. They can act just like "D"s if pushed into a corner, especially if it affects their security. "S" service personnel are the most gentle and accommodating. They tend to be taken advantage of and need to be stronger with those who intimidate them. Everyone should learn from "S"s when it comes to staying calm and genuinely trying to make customers happy.

"C" types: "C"s can be the most picky customers. They drive service personnel crazy with the fine print. "C" service personnel come across as unbending. They need to be more tolerant and understanding. "C" customers, dealing with "C" service personnel, can get into heated debates over right or wrong. Of course, "the customer is always right!" — even when the "C" service personnel knows the customer is really wrong.

NOTE: Service personnel need to deal with each customer according to their personalities. For instance, help the "D" quickly and respectfully. Service the "I" friendly and enthusiastically. Respond to the "S" with sweetness and security. And service the "C" customer with patience and answers.

Dealing With Objections

Every personality responds predictably under pressure. Overcoming objections is every seller's greatest challenge. Sellers need to know how to deal with objections according to personality types. The following are suggestions to help change an objection into a positive decision.

"D" Types

"D" sellers will predictably respond in a strong and difficult way. They tend to resist with a seemingly angry attitude. Instead of challenging "D"s to "take-it or leave-it," they should be given the opportunity to be part of a difficult challenge or project. Or "D"s should be encouraged to consider the consequences if they make the wrong decision. "D"s need choices, plus alternative ways to get out of difficult situations. Show them how their decision can make them more successful.

"I" Types

"I"s often think they can do more than they are capable. When confronted with reality, they may be embarrassed and object to the conclusion. Wise sellers will never press the problem. These types quickly change direction and find another positive approach of influencing the "I" types. When "I"s continue to object, attention should be shifted to the buyer's prestige and how purchasing your product will also make them look good.

"S" Types

"S" buyers withdraw when confronted with difficult decisions. Their objections will range from "let me think about it" to "I'm not ready to decide yet." The seller's soft answer and relaxed attitude helps "S"s feel more comfortable. Wise sellers should use statements like, "We want a long range relationship with you" and "We're in no hurry to make you decide now." But wise leaders will still try to move "S" followers to make good decisions without being pushy.

"C" Types

"C"s are the most challenging when it comes to objections. The best approach is using quality and value to help them decide. When a "C" says, "I'm not interested," leaders should emphasize a logical reason why purchasing a product is best. For example, emphasize the cost for purchasing the product now will be less than in the future. "C"s should be reminded how much more waiting will cost. It is only logical to go ahead and buy now.

First Signs / Non-Verbal Communication

People often reveal their personalities through body language. Their nonverbal communication helps sellers know how to approach them. Each personality type has its own body language. Sellers should look for the first signs of a follower's predictable pattern of behavior.

The following are examples of specific personality hints. I will use an automobile dealership situation to illustrate each personality's typical body language.

"D" Types

"D"s look busy, in a hurry, and decisive. They act serious with minimal small-talk. They may come across as shy, but can become very impatient and fidgety if nothing seems to be happening. They take charge and act important. Others are often threatened or irritated by "D"s, but need to work with them, not against them. Let them feel they are the "boss" and in control of the situation.

"I" Types

"I"s like to smile, laugh, and tell funny stories. They often dress nice and look sharp. They like bright clothes and seek compliments. They are articulate and impress others. Their exciting and enthusiastic demeanor often makes great first impressions. They are very friendly and sociable. They drop names and sometimes exaggerate their stories. "I"s tend to be loud and take over conversations.

"S" Types

"S"s walk into a room often unsure of themselves. They look sheepish and shy. They like to blend in without any attention on themselves. "S"s come across very caring and kind. They may seem antisocial, but are very friendly one-on-one. They seek steady and stable environments. "S"s do not talk much in a large group. They often ask questions about families and the interests of others.

"C" Types

"C" often look like the professor type. They are not that concerned about fashion. "C"s look serious and disinterested in fanfare. They do not care about frills or thrills. They seem to catch inconsistent or exaggerated statements. With an inquisitive look and suspicious mind, "C"s come across as a hard to get to know.

They are often knowledgeable with lots of questions or opinions about most subjects.

Business Builder Styles

Everyone has a predictable pattern of behavior. Being able to read these styles will improve your effectiveness in whatever you do. The most important lesson to learn is how to adapt your personality type to that of the person you are trying to influence.

The key is understanding how each personality type naturally responds. As a Business Builder you have a specific style. If not careful, you will work the same way to everyone.

Though other people may never change, your style in leading them must be flexible. Do not think every one will always respond the same. People respond according to their specific personality types. The wise Business Builder learns to adapt to the personality of others.

For example, when recruiting a "D" type, if you are an "I" type, do not expect the person to be interested in "chit chat." He or she will want you to get to the point. Do not beat around the bush. Ask for a decision as soon as you have clearly presented the opportunity. Expect resistance. A "D" will challenge you. Do not be threatened. Be strong and serious.

If you are a "D" sharing with an "I" do not expect the person to respond to a direct presentation. "Chit chat" for a while. Do not get to the point right away. Take your time. Let them talk. Your challenge will be listening to "I"s while they get side tracked with their stories. Be enthusiastic and excited about the opportunities.

The following are specific Business Builder styles:

"D" Types

Domineering and demanding Business Builders can be extremely effective. They are self-starters with a sense of urgency. But their driving concern to succeed can make them too pushy. "D" Business Builders should be more gentle and patient. Determined to get the job done, they often feel like everyone should be involved in their dream. Direct with their presentations, they like leaders who are results-oriented. Potential "D" Business Builders are hard workers, but often difficult to convince. Once convinced and focused, they very do well.

"I" Types

Influencing type Business Builders are the most enthusiastic. They are also very contagious — company cheerleaders. Interested in people, they are "natural-born" salespeople. "I"s make sharing the presentation look so easy. Because of their strong desire to impress, they may care equally about what people think of them and recruiting success. They must constantly remember that they are not as important as helping others. Once properly trained and determined not to get side-tracked, "I" Business Builders are often the most effective.

"S" Types

Sweet and soft type Business Builders are the most gentle leaders. They recruit and share slowly, but steadily. They do not like to force issues. They tend to be too nice. "Doubters" often waste "S"s' time. Knowing "S"s will go the extra mile, some people take advantage. Avoiding confrontation, "S" Business Builders prefer to only share and speak with close friends. But their motivation to succeed can often overcome their natural reluctance to speak out.

"S"s Business Builders are the slowest starters, but most faithful and consistent.

"C" Types

Cautious and compliant type Business Builders are the most thorough and knowledgeable. They like to go point-by-point, convincing people to understand every detail. They try to have an answer for every question. But they can overwhelm others with too many facts. "C"s are often more concerned with the task, rather than the person in need. As competent individuals, they need to be more flexible and friendly. "C"s turn doubt into fascinating opportunities, once convinced themselves. They prefer a lot of learning resources, but need to go with less.

Insights For Leaders Of Business Builder

Independence and building your own business can be very exciting and / or scary. Nearly everyone wants to be his or her own boss. There is a specific personality type that is determined to control his or her destiny. There are other types content with being told what to do and following orders for the rest of their lives.

Maturity and experience often influence the most reluctant personalities. They need to stretch their horizons and investigate the possibilities of being self-employed. There are tremendous advantages with operating your own business. You can be the boss. You have charge over your schedule. You can take days or weeks off without permission. Your income and freedom are unlimited. The advantages of being a business builder are endless.

The problem is most people do not understand the "Science of

Motivation." They do not realize everyone *is* already motivated. Some people are motivated to be free from control, while others are motivated and satisfied to be told what to do. But everyone is motivated!

Once we understand what makes us tick and what gets us ticking, we can become more productive in whatever we do. The most important lesson is learning how to control our personalities and motivations, rather than letting our natural drives control us.

The following are insights about how different personality types respond as business builders. Certain types tend to start stronger, but fail faster. Other personalities start slower, but can be very successful. Study each of the following personality types to learn how to be more effective.

Remember, everyone can be a successful business builder!

"D" Business Builders

Indicators:
- Wants to be own boss
- Failed in other attempts, but is not discouraged
- Interested in high income potential
- Independent
- Impatient
- Aggressive
- Fearless
- Self-starter

Do:
- Give "bottom line" / direct answers
- Give specific guidelines
- Vision of what can be achieved

- Simple steps to get started, instead of letting run free and careless.
- Be realistic

Don't:
- Try to control
- Speak down or baby him or her
- Exaggerate expected results
- Encourage going into debt
- Quit "day job"
- Doubt or discourage high goals

Needs To Learn:
- How to follow the rules
- To be a team player
- To control aggressiveness
- To be more patient and understanding
- To take smaller steps
- To take time to improve product knowledge and study product
- Information

"I" Business Builders

Indicators:
- Talks a lot
- Loves to travel and have fun
- Has lots of friends
- Is enthusiastic
- Optimistic
- Active
- Outgoing

- Sociable
- Influential
- Often well-liked

Do:
- Share the possibilities and potential enthusiastically
- Often stroke and approve
- Recognize accomplishments
- Stress rewards — bonus cars, travel, conventions, and fun.

Don't:
- Believe everything
- Bank on promises
- Overwhelm with information
- Stress paperwork and details
- Expect punctuality
- Criticize
- Be negative

Needs To Learn:
- Great expectations should begin with hard work and less talk
- Product knowledge is important
- To take time to do the little and mundane things
- Follow through with plans
- Be consistent
- Stay focused
- To follow-up with people

"S" Business Builders

Indicators:
- Is quiet
- Reserved

- Good listener
- Not outspoken
- Slow to respond
- Not often enthusiastic
- Sensitive
- Shy
- Faithful
- Dependable
- Passive
- Steady
- Family-oriented

Do:

- Take it slow
- Share with more sincerity and less hype
- Respect family responsibilities
- Show interest in lasting relationship more than just business interest
- Give confidence

Don't:

- Push too fast
- Give up
- Expect instant results
- Set goals too high
- Allow doubt and fear to stifle
- Share difficulties without assurance of constant support
- Leave alone and don't be pushy

Needs To Learn:

- Achievement is possible

- To be a self-starter
- Be more enthusiastic
- To dream big
- To initiate conversation
- Take risks
- To challenge others
- To take charge
- Be bold and aggressive
- Most people may not respond well, but many will

"C" Business Builders

Indicators:

- Asks lots of questions
- Is cautious
- Doubting
- Researching
- Analytical
- Wants details
- Thorough
- Not real friendly
- Wants to do one thing at a time
- Does things right

Do:

- Be patient with questions
- Give detailed answers
- Encourage to be more sociable; to get started
- Provide lots of product information
- Emphasize quality and research

Don't:
- Give incorrect or unfounded answers
- Expect instant responses
- Be silly
- Give up because of pessimistic attitude
- Demand cheerleader type responses
- Avoid difficult questions

Needs To Learn:
- To be more optimistic
- Get started with little information
- Not to worry
- To be more outgoing
- To be friendly
- Share information with enthusiasm
- To turn research into results
- To spend time with people

Insights For Business Builder

Every Business Builder has a specific style in sharing his or her presentation. Potential team members also have specific personality types that respond well or poorly. Certain styles conflict. Success is hindered when Business Builders and target individuals clash. Identifying predictable styles will improve your results.

No style is better than the other. The wise Business Builder responds according to the other person's style. Unfortunately, many people do not know their Business Building style. They also do not know how to read and identify the personality types of others.

Sharing with friends is also difficult. Familiarity often breeds contempt. In other words, the closer you get, the easier it is to conflict. The things we often love about someone, we sometimes come to despise. Understanding styles of behavior will help you deal with the differences between you and others. Be sure to identify both personalities.

When an aggressive Business Builder shares with a passive individual, do not think he or she will respond just like you did. Learn to deal with the individual according to his or her specific personality. It is your responsibility to adapt and guide the situation. You are the "host" and they are the "guests."

The following are proven and practical ways to deal with different types of personalities. Focus on your D, I, S or C type, along with that of another individual. Be sure to consider your Behavioral Blend and other predominant temperament tendencies ("highs").

"D" Trying To Recruit and / or Lead

"D": Be strong, but willing to bend. The "D" will challenge and intimidate you. Get to the point. Remind him or her that this challenge has tremendous rewards.

"I": Be enthusiastic and complimentary. The "I" will talk and exaggerate a lot. Listen and do not try to control the conversation or steamroll him or her.

"S": Be sweet. Do not be forceful or speak down. The "S" will judge how you respond. Be sensitive and kind. Appreciate the "S"s' relational concerns.

"C": Be prepared. Do not use generalities. Be specific. The "C" wants thorough explanation, not shallow answers. A "C" will resist if you do not know your subject.

"I" Trying To Recruit and / or Lead

"D": Be serious. Do not be silly or informal. The "D" person is not interested in funny stories. Do not waste time. Express the opportunity to be your own boss.

"I": Be a good listener. Do not talk much. Compliment the "I". Emphasize the good and positive. Smile and agree, as much as possible.

"S": Be sensitive. Let the "S" share his or her feelings. Do not interrupt. Reinforce your commitment to help. Stay calm. Show warmth and sensitivity.

"C": Be factual. Do not "snow" the "C". Ask exploratory questions. Be open and respectful. Give details. Be precise and methodical.

"S" Trying To Recruit and / or Lead

"D": Be confident and sure of yourself. The "D" may be forceful. Be strong and bold. Challenge the "D", but not too hard. Do not show timidity.

"I": Be interested in what the "I" says. Do not just listen. Share your thoughts and concerns. Tell the "I" how exciting it is to be a part of this venture. Be enthusiastic.

"S": Be kind, but do not overdo it. Be strong, if necessary. Do not hold back, but be sensitive. Encourage the "S" to respond now. Share how much it has helped you.

"C": Be ready for questions. The "C" will pressure you with logic. Do not condemn his or her doubts. Give concrete answers. Give him or her time to decide.

"C" Trying To Recruit and / or Lead

"D": Be relaxed. Do not be defensive. Get to the "bottom line." Do not bore the "D" with a lot of facts. Agree on solution based on other perspectives. Be positive.

"I": Be patient. Let the "I" talk. Be enthusiastic about the opportunities — travel, bonus cars, meeting new friends. Get the "I" to talk through to the solution. Stay on track.

"S": Be loving. Show sincere care for the "S". Make the "S" feel you really enjoy what you do. Do not complain. Be optimistic and sure of your plan.

"C": Be precise and accurate. Meet forceful demands with clear answers. Be sure of your facts. Be open to suggestions. Offer information and resources to study.

Recruiting / Prospecting Insights

Prospecting to find new customers or clients is often the hardest part of any project. Understanding personality types can make you more effective as a "motivator." We often waste precious time with those who will never respond or we give up too quickly with potentially great workers. The following are simple suggestions to help in prospecting according to personality types. Remember, the recruiter must adapt his or her personality to those being recruited.

"D" types: "D"s tend to be pushy in their approach. They also resist or respond quickly. If you are a "D" type, be more patient and gentle. When recruiting "D"s, get to the point. Do not waste their time. Quickly show them the potential and power of the program. Expect an immediate response, but do not argue with them. Stress how the program allows them to be their own boss and reach their goals in life.

"I" types: "I"s make the most enthusiastic recruiters. They are also the quickest to respond positively and aggressively. They need to be more informed, or they will give exaggerated statements and false claims. "I"s should concentrate on the details. Be sure to give "I"s accurate information. They also need periodic "pumping up." It does not take much, but good news is contagious to "I"s.

"S" types: "S" are more steady recruiters. They systematically work at building relationships and convincing others to get involved. When recruiting "S"s, be more kind and loving. They appreciate when you call to just talk and not "ask" them for anything. They are very loyal, but not outwardly expressive. They are slow to decide and need a lot of assurance. Once convinced they make hard workers.

"C" types: "C"s are the most thorough and conscientious recruiters. They sometimes get bogged down with preparation and never get off the ground. When recruiting "C"s, understand they

are the most skeptical. You can waste a lot of time trying to convince them. It is often best to simply supply them with literature. Let them study the facts. When convinced they make surprisingly good optimists.

Memory Jogger / Prospects List

Focus on each category listed next. Take a moment to think of someone who comes to mind. Write his or her name down to contact ASAP. You basically have two choices: (1) wait for opportunities to just happen or (2) make them happen. Success comes as you plan your work and work your plan.

Building your business is easier when you understand ...

1. People You Work With
2. Boss
3. Partner
4. Trainer
5. Landlord
6. Security Guard
7. Supervisor
8. Secretary
9. Typing Pool
10. Caterer
11. Customers
12. Parking Attendant
13. Coffee Shop
14. Car Pool
15. Mentor
16. Salesperson
17. Mortgage Broker
18. Lunch With
19. Courier
20. Repair Person
21. Copier Repair Person
22. Union People
23. Homemaker
24. Office In Home
25. Credit Union
26. Pension Plan
27. Sports Fan
28. Door-to-door Sales
29. Delivery Person
30. Federal Express
31. U.P.S.

32. Mail Person
33. Soon To Graduate
34. Almost Lost Job
35. Will Be Laid Off
36. Unemployed
37. Dissatisfied With Job
38. Searching For Career
39. Switching Careers
40. Missed Last Promotion
41. Walking Encyclopedia
42. Most Likable
43. Needs Part-time Job
44. Engineer
45. New Employee
46. Human Resource Director
47. Payroll
48. Contractor
49. Sales Manager
50. Marketing Manager
51. Minister / Clergy
52. Nurse
53. Dentist
54. Doctor
55. Surgeon
56. Chiropractor
57. Therapist
58. Carpenter
59. Auto Mechanic
60. Auto Salesperson
61. Auto Body Repair
62. Service Station

63. Former Coach	94. Dry Cleaner
64. Educator	95. Radio Shack
65. Banker	96. TV Repair
66. Teller	97. Mail Room
67. Police Officer	98. Video Rental
68. Highway Patrol	99. Appliance Person
69. Home Builder	100. Cable TV
70. Painter	101. Eye Center
71. Roofer	102. Tire Store
72. Entrepreneur	103. Realtor
73. Landscaper	104. Office Supplies
74. Wallpaper Person	105. Copier Salesperson
75. Carpet Layer	106. Vacuum Cleaner
76. Hospital Worker	107. Phone Installer
77. Department Store	108. Pest Control Person
78. Grocery Store	109. Avon Representative
79. Convenient Store	110. Nu-Skin
80. Waitress / Waiter	111. Melaleuca
81. Restaurant Owner	112. Amway / Quixtar
82. Chef / Cook	113. Appliance Repair
83. Cashier	114. Bowl With
84. Telemarketer	115. Hunt With
85. Auto Supply	116. Golf With
86. Electrician	117. Fish With
87. Hardware Store	118. Tennis With
88. Truck Driver	119. Ski With
89. Pharmacist	120. Shop With
90. Funeral Director	121. Softball With
91. Flower Shop	122. Baseball With
92. Health Spa	123. Football With
93. Shoe Repair	124. Soccer With

125. Racquetball With
126. Aerobics With
127. Swim With
128. Public Official
129. Fire Person
130. Government Worker
131. Scout Master
132. Den Leader
133. Barber
134. Beautician
135. Home Repair
136. Entertainer
137. Musician
138. Photographer
139. Guidance Counselor
140. Youth Director
141. Sister-in-law
142. Brother-in-law
143. Father-in-law
144. Mother-in-law
145. Brother
146. Sister
147. Father
148. Mother
149. Cousin
150. Aunt
151. Uncle
152. Grandfather
153. Grandmother
154. Niece
155. Nephew

156. Best Friend
157. Mate's Best Friend
158. Farmer
159. Army Person
160. Navy Person
161. Air Force Person
162. Marines Person
163. Baby-sitter
164. Step-relatives
165. Neighbors
166. Pizza Delivery Person
167. Homeowners Assoc.
168. Neighborhood Watch
169. Square Dances
170. Line Dances
171. Ballroom Dances
172. Best Man
173. Maid of Honor
174. Matron of Honor
175. Bridesmaids
176. Ushers
177. Church Members
178. Plumber
179. Carpet Cleaner
180. Play Bridge / Cards
181. Play Bingo
182. Play Pool
183. Play Ping-pong
184. Trivial Pursuit
185. Booster Club
186. Runner / Jogger

187. Boater
188. Cyclist
189. Recreation Director
190. Rock/Mt. Climber
191. Hang Glider
192. Walker
193. PTA
194. Principal
195. Teacher
196. Coach
197. Music Teacher
198. Piano Teacher
199. Fraternity Brother
200. Sorority Sister
201. Former Team Mate
202. Former Associate
203. Instructor
204. Lamaze Class
205. Kiwanis
206. Lions Club
207. Rotary
208. Support Group
209. Friend's Parents
210. Grade School Friend
211. Lawyer
212. Highway Department
213. Professor
214. Sunday School
215. Chamber of Commerce
216. Hotel Business
217. Printer

218. Surveyor
219. Nutritionist
220. Writer / Author
221. Rental Supply
222. Book Store
223. Tanning Salon
224. Jeweler
225. Baker
226. Librarian
227. Accountant
228. Pilot
229. Flight Attendant
230. Travel Agent
231. Store Owner
232. Telephone Operator
233. Choir / Band Director
234. Church Deacon/Leader
235. Seminar Presenter
236. Camp With
237. Locksmith
238. Upholsterer
239. Veterinarian
240. Notary Public
241. Orthodontist
242. Dance Instructor
243. Moved In Neighborhood
244. Recently Divorced
245. Computer Programmer
246. Computer Repair
247. Computer Sales
248. C.P.A.

249. Bookkeeper
250. Architect
251. Landscaper
252. Cab Driver
253. Bus Driver
254. Cat Lover
255. Dog Lover
256. Horse Lover
257. Animal Trainer
258. Social Worker
259. Seamstress
260. Home / Garden Supply
261. Likes To Sing
262. Likes To Eat

263. Likes To Talk
264. Insurance Salesperson
265. Stock Broker
266. Former Neighbor
267. Receptionist
268. Janitor
269. Rich Relative
270. Ex-mate
271. Health Food Shop
272. Hobby Shop
273. Hotel / Motel Operator
274. Pet Store
275. Tax Preparer
276. Internet Technician

It may seem like this list can go on and on. Actually it could. Everyone you know or meet is a potential customer or can help you find one. If you do not think people will be interested in your business, simply ask if they know of someone that may be interested.

The problem is that most people are passive and do not want to "pressure" anyone by asking for his or her help. Some people are aggressive and do not mind asking. If you are more shy, my question to you is: are going to let your personality control you or are you going to control your personality?

If you are passive, "get over it!" Better yet, I should appeal to your sweet and sensitive personality by supporting you and sharing how much I believe that you can build your business, and I should reason with you and convince you that it can be done. But you know what I am doing right now. I just want you to get out of the trap and pitfall of your own personality.

If One Million Dollars Can Be Yours!

What if I offered you a million dollars to ask people to help you? If you say, you still would not do it, what about five million, or ten million? How much would it take? If you say you would not be aggressive and outgoing to build your business for all the money in the world, then that is your choice.

What if your child was dying from a rare disease? What would you do? I have seen so many passive people who became very assertive and active when it came to helping their families. Everything has its price. What is it that will motivate you to get out of your comfort zone and shell to be your own boss and build your business? It *is* your choice, so what's my point?

Just do it! I originally thought the Nike's advertisement campaign was designed for "D"s and "I"s, but the more I thought about it, I realized it was especially good for "S"s and "C"s. The "Just Do It!" idea is for all you "S" types who do not think you *can* do it, whatever "it" is, and it is for all you "C" types who waste a lot of your time trying to figure out what "it" is. Just do it! The IT is building your business with the determination of a "D," the inspiration of an "I," the stability of an "S," and competence of a "C" type.

Stop making excuses and just do it! That is my obvious "D" point! So, what's your point?

Point #8

Be healthy, wealthy, and wise by controlling your motivations!

"Be healthy, wealthy, and wise" is not just a famous saying. It is a smart motto to live by. What is the alternative — being sickly, poor, and foolish? I am not implying that sickly people are poor or foolish. Many people suffer from poor health that they cannot control. But more people suffer because of unwise decisions they have made over the years.

Being unhealthy is also expensive. Taking care of yourself is one of your wisest investments. Why you do what you do is so important to being healthy, wealthy, and wise. Your motivations often affect your decisions and your personality often affects your motivations.

How you get, guard, and give your money is also part of being healthy, wealthy, and wise. The same is true for how you use your time. Being a good manager of your health, money, and time will definitely determine your success in life. The following are vital insights to help you identify and control your motivations when it comes to your health, money, and time.

Why Wellness?

Wellness is not an option! Taking care of ourselves must be a priority, if we want to enjoy life to its fullest. Especially with so many unknowns and pressures today, we must desperately guard our health. Wellness must be an essential part of our everyday way of life. We cannot afford to think that physical and financial security are luxuries. They are investments. Staying healthy is less expensive than staying unhealthy.

Taking care of yourself is one of the wisest investments of your life. The problem with getting and staying healthy is that it takes personal motivation. Why we do what we do is one of the determining factors to our success. Our motivation affects our eating habits, exercising, and investing in food supplements.

Motivation affects everything we do!

Motivation is a mystery to most people. There is also a myth and misunderstanding about motivation. The myth of motivation is thinking that people are not already motivated. The truth is, everybody is motivated. Some people are motivated to do one thing, while others are motivated to do the exact opposite. But everyone is motivated. The question is: "What motivates us?"

Some people are motivated to be healthy, because they want to be strong. They want to be in control of themselves. Others are motivated to be healthy, because they want to look great and make good impressions. Others are motivated to be healthy, because it is more safe and secure. They do not like trouble or change. They like steady environments. Others are motivated because it is logical and wise to take care of themselves. They look at wellness as the right thing to do.

Our motivations obviously affect our wellness. It is natural to be healthy and it is unnatural to be unhealthy. Nature responds to our motivations. Everything in life runs down, unless we take care of it. The Law of Entropy warns us about decay and disease. Energy, in any given system, always runs toward randomness and chaos when left alone.

Wellness doesn't just happen. It takes effort!

We must have a plan to stay fit. If not, the eventual decline is inevitable! Lack of wellness runs toward ruin. Lack of motivation ends in a wasted life. By recognizing your motivations from a personality perspective, you can guard your strengths and avoid your weaknesses. Once you identify your specific personality profile, you can then learn how to improve your motivations.

Your personality profile is designed to help you understand why you do what you do when it comes to your health. Human Behavior Science can improve your motivations toward a more healthy life. Identifying your personality, in light of your motivations, can be extremely beneficial.

Your health and future are important. Take the time to understand why you do what you do. Learn how to improve the quality of your life. Do it for yourself and loved ones. There is nothing wrong with taking care of yourself.

It is essential that you take the time to understand your motivations and improve your health. It can be the beginning of a whole new way of thinking, feeling, and acting. It can add years to your life, and life to your years! Wellness is more than just wise living, It can also be your way to health and happiness!

Health Factors

There are three vital factors to the success or failure of your health — diet, exercise, and food supplements. Together, they make the difference in the quality of your life. Some people are fortunate and being overweight is never a problem. But everyone needs to watch what they eat. Just because you do not gain weight, you should still be careful what you put into your body.

Food is energy. You should supply your body with the best energy sources available. Proper exercise is also essential. Regular exercise strengthens and tones your muscles to help them receive the full nutrients in the foods you eat. Eating right without exercise is like fueling a magnificent engine without enjoying its power. Eating right and exercising regularly are not enough to attain optimal health.

In this world of processed foods and chemical substitutes, we must add the specific nutrients our bodies need. It is not enough to guard against eating the wrong foods, we must also supplement our diets with the minerals and vitamins that are lost in the process of our "instant everything" world. We often respond to these three factors — diet, exercise, and food supplements — according to our personalities. Understanding our predictable patterns of behavior can help us guard our strengths and avoid our weaknesses.

Study the following insights to improve your motivations. Always remember, you are the only one who can motivate yourself to do right. Do not expect or depend on anyone else to give you the determination to respond appropriately. Learn to control your personality, rather than letting your personality control you. Take command of your feelings and thinking to control your craving and lack of discipline.

"D" Behavior

Dieting

Is often too busy to take the time. Is easily sidetracked by "more important" things. Once committed, is determined and disciplined. Starts strong, but lacks follow through. Needs accountability and regimentation. Does best when challenged.

Exercising

Wants independence and power to work alone. Motivated by challenge and need to be strong. Is serious and determined, but often falls short of potential. Does best as a leader or example.

Nutritional Supplements

Often underestimates need. Thinks he or she is strong enough. Does not want to think about it. Does not like the routine. Once convinced, is driven and direct. Does best when reminded of the "bottom line."

"I" Behavior

Dieting

Is extremely conscious of how he or she looks. Wants to impress others, but compensates for overeating by being the life of the party. Eating and socializing are important; should be done with moderation. Needs to discipline lack of control and desire to feel good by overeating.

Exercising

Is initially enthusiastic, but lacks follow through. Loves to exercise with a group. The more the merrier. At best when able to influence others. Needs to stick with it, even when it is not fun any more.

Nutritional Supplements

Using supplements can be difficult, because it is so routine and mundane. Must control forgetfulness with set patterns and conscious efforts, because of the ultimate results — better health and happiness.

"S" Behavior

Dieting

Can be most consistent and yet, least motivated. Is often insecure with dieting and slow getting started. Can be influenced by a close friend, but needs to be more self motivated. Does best once routine is established and sure of method of dieting.

Exercising

Does not need a lot of hype. Is content to work alone, but does best with a friend. Does not push the limits as much as they should, but is better at the long haul. Is steady and regimented, but needs to control interruptions.

Nutritional Supplements

Is the best at taking food supplements once convinced with the need and a schedule is established. Needs to guard against always taking same or cheap food supplements without researching to find the best.

"C" Behavior

Dieting

Very conscious of weight. Often worries about being overweight, but is more likely to act on it. Can get easily discouraged and give up too soon. Needs to be more optimistic about possibilities and begin dieting immediately. Should not spend too much time researching every diet plan.

Exercising

Very calculating and studious. Wants the best plan. Can be too serious and regimented. Needs to relax and have more fun. Can be too hard on him or herself. Is often best at knowing what to do, but has poor attitude about doing it.

Nutritional Supplements

A stickler for details. Needs to know scientific facts first. Is often skeptical, but once convinced is consistent. Often procrastinates, because of need for more data. Struggles with "just doing it," but when committed does it well.

Balancing Your Health

You are what you eat! It is an old saying and is more important today than ever. Exercise and nutritional supplements also affect your health. Everywhere you look there is growing concern over how to improve your fitness. Understanding your personality is important to how you take care of yourself. Just as there are different personalities, there are different wellness motivators. The following is a basic look at the four temperaments and how to improve your health and fitness.

"D" Type

Your active / task-oriented life style makes you a determined, doer, and driver type. You tend to eat to live, not live to eat. You are often "too busy" to take better care of yourself.

Think it over

- Control your motivation to be constantly busy.
- Determine to take care of your health and fitness.
- Discipline your time and energy so that you exercise and eat well.
- Guard against being constantly on the go.
- Schedule time to "stop and smell the roses."
- Do not let your need to stay busy keep you from rest.

"I" Type

Your active / people-oriented life style causes you to constantly be on the go. You are prone to eat on the run. You enjoy meal time best when it becomes a social event.

Think it over

- Let your motivation to impress and inspire others influence how you eat.
- Discipline cravings by reminding yourself how overeating will make you look poor.
- Keep nutritional low-fat energy snacks available for when you become hungry.
- Resist fast foods.
- Avoid grocery shopping when you are hungry.

"S" Type

Your passive / people-oriented life style makes you a submissive, sensitive, and soft type person. You tend to be more consistent with your diet, whether it be a good or bad diet. You do not like change.

Think it over

- Be careful you do not get into the rut of eating the same unhealthy foods all the time.
- Avoid your reluctance to change.
- Do not let other people decide what you should eat.
- Be different when others want greasy fast foods.
- Be assertive and order or cook healthy foods.
- Develop a healthy diet and exercise program that you will stick to no matter what your friends do.

"C" Type

Your passive / task-oriented life style makes you more calculating and competent. You can be "picky" about what you eat, but can become defeated by discouragement and then give in to your cravings.

Think it over

- Control your emotions and do not let difficulties cause you to give up on eating well.
- Let your analytical thinking decide what is best to eat and how to exercise.
- Get excited about looking good and feeling better.
- Do not accept the status quo, if change is necessary.
- Challenge yourself through wise reason to take better care of your body.

• Do not think that preserving your mind is more important than taking care of your body.

Exercise For All Types

Everyone needs twenty-five to sixty minutes of rhythmic exercise, three to six times a week, to keep your body chemistry balanced. Aerobic (cardiovascular conditioning), strength training, and flexibility exercises are vital to maintaining good health.

Foods For All Types

Fruits, vegetables, whole grain cereals, rice, pasta, white and pink fish, white poultry (skinless), high fiber (beans & whole wheat bread), lean protein (eggs), nonfat or low-fat dairy, and nuts.

Supplements For All Types

Soy Protein; Multivitamins with the right amounts of vitamins A, B6, B12, C, E, D, K, Thiamin, Riboflavin, Niacin, Folic Acid, Biotin, Panthothenic Acid, Iron, Calcium, Phosphorus, Magnesium, Zinc, Selenium, Copper, Manganese, Chromium, Molybdenum, Nickel, Tin, Vanadium, Boron, Silicon, plus other minerals; EPA, Alfalfa, Glucosamine, GLA, St. John's Wort, Echinacea, Ginkgo, Peppermint Ginger, and Garlic.

I'm going to add another important factor to improve your health. Mental Attitude is so important. An ancient proverb says, "you are what you think!"

Mental Attitude For All Types

Think more positively; Look at problems as potential blessings; Think on things that are pure, good, and virtuous; accept failure as an opportunity for change; laugh more; Don't Worry - Be Happy; be more optimistic and trusting; be careful, but enthusiastic.

All Supplements are NOT Alike!

You deserve better than brand X. With so many supplements flooding the market, there is a serious need to be more cautious. The FDA (Federal Drug Administration) does not guarantee any vitamin. It usually does not get involved until something goes wrong. Some vitamins do not dissolve in our system in time to do us any good. Vital nutrients may never make it into our blood stream. We literally flush money down the toilet!

It is our responsibility to tell the truth about supplements. We must warn you about the misrepresentation and abuse of vitamins. The old covered-wagon "snake oil salesman" is alive and well today. Health and cure claims are running wild. People are desperate to believe anything. Because of our commitment to truth and quality, we only recommend all natural supplements. The claim that synthetic vitamins are just as good as true natural vitamins is a scientific deception.

We recommend only **Shaklee Products** for several reasons. First of all, people often ask us what products we recommend. We cannot, in good conscience, recommend that anyone purchase other products because we do not know or trust their research and development, or the manufacturing of the other products. Also for liability sake we only recommend Shaklee's 50 years of experience and impeccable integrity in the nutritional industry.

Shaklee's products are in **Harmony With Nature and Good Health**® because they are the result of a painstaking process of scientific review and assessment of third-party research and independent clinical studies. Each product must perform to a standard of excellence. Each product must deliver the correct dosage of key ingredients, based on clinical research.

If you would like to know more about Shaklee's products, go to *www.shaklee.com* or to find a distributor near you, go to *www.shaklee.net* and click on ***Find a Distributor***.

To hear an exciting and brief recorded message from Shaklee's owner and CEO, Roger Barnett, phone 1-925-924-3333.

Maintaining Good Health

The bottom line is "what do you believe and how do you act about wellness from a personal perspective?" Are you like so many religious or non-religious people today, wanting to take better care of your body, but feeling guilty about your weight or overall health? Or are you concerned about your family and friends who are suffering physically?

Wellness is really about the choices we make every day. Many people are in bondage to poor health habits. Even most ministries today preach a lot about the soul and spirit, but neglect teaching about the *body*. Let this be a ***Call To Commitment*** to practice what you believe about taking care of your temple. If you are a non-religious person, you still have an obligation to yourself, family and job to maintain good health.

One of the purposes for discovering your personality is to help you examine yourself, your home, work and faith; to learn how to improve your effectiveness through better physical, nutritional, mental, emotional, social and spiritual health. Being introduced to this may be providential. It may be your wake-up call. You may be sincerely trying to do your best, but are struggling with the whole health issue. Let us help you bring all this to a serious conclusion.

The following admonitions may save your life or the life of a friend, family member, or associate. Take heed or suffer the consequences!

Nutritional & Physical Health

What you do with your body will determine what your body will do for you! You *must* first feed your body with the best premium fuel you can afford. Former Surgeon General C. Everett Koop states: "If you do not smoke or drink excessively, your diet can influence your long-term health prospects more than any other action you might take."

If necessary, change your eating habits. Also, supplementation is no longer an option. Begin taking the best quality vitamins and minerals. You can not afford not to. You will pay the price one way or the other. Like someone said, "Pay for it now or pay for it later" (through higher medical bills).

Exercise is also a must. The older you get the more important it is. Especially concentrate on three types of exercises:

(1) Cardio-vascular exercises that get your heart beating fast for 20 - 30 minutes per day.

(2) Stretching exercises that help your muscles and joints stay young.

(3) Strengthening exercises that keep your muscles toned and flexible.

Mental & Emotional Health

Your mind and motivations are perhaps your greatest areas to guard. It is not always what you are eating that is most important. Sometimes it is what is eating you. Your attitude and positive perspective on life are tremendous protective and healing agents. Guard your mind and emotions from constant negativism.

Determine before every meal or snack that you are going to exchange the short-lived feeling of satisfaction with the discipline of what is best for your body. You can feel good for a little while overeating and eating the wrong things, or you can feel better longer by cutting back on your portions and eating the proper foods.

Control your feelings and cravings by being determined and stronger mentally. Substitute your cravings with your commitment to your own well-being!

Social & Spiritual Health

Relationships are so important to a healthy life. Work on improving your relationship with others by spending quality time with both. It is not enough to simply cohabitate, you must communicate better. Try improving your listening skills. Be less or more assertive based on your DISC personality type. Be more or less expressive than what comes naturally.

Cultivating good relations is like working a garden. Keep the weeds out, water regularly, and fertilize with organic nutrients. It takes time and effort, but you will reap rewarding results if you take it seriously. Do it for your faith, your family, and yourself.

Suggested Self-Affirmation Commitment

"I am special. I recognize I was created to enjoy life to its fullest. I acknowledge that taking care of my body, soul, and spirit should be priorities, not to worship my body or be proud of my accomplishments, but to reap the benefits and blessings of a disciplined life!

I know I have been given the strength and will to do what I should. I will, from this day forward, begin eating better foods, supplementing my meals with nutritional supplements, exercising adequately, thinking more positively, controlling my feelings and cravings, plus improving my relationships with others!"

Signed _____

How DISC Personality Types GET Their Money

It is not wrong to have money. What matters is what we do with it! Your personality type will affect how you get, guard, and give away your money. The following are simple insights to help you manage your finances from your personality perspective. Keep in mind your primary and secondary temperament types.

Study all the pages to learn more about how all 4 DISC personality types relate to resource mangers. These insights are especially designed to help you and others understand how to be good managers of your resources.

"D" TYPE RESOURCE MANAGERS

In A Word: Diligent – "Work for it!"

Abilities: They are more risk-takers in investing or starting new businesses. They are hard workers and will work long hours. They tend to never be satisfied with enough. Using multiple streams of income is one of their goals.

Strategies: Remember to make honesty a primary strategy for acquiring money. Teamwork makes the dream work so work with others and keep them informed. Redirect your drive to succeed in accomplishing greater tasks with the determination to save, save, save, and save some more.

Warning: Keep a budget. Decide when "enough is enough." Be content with what you have. Do not sacrifice time with your family and worship by working so hard to get more money. Remember the purpose of acquiring resources is to meet the basic needs of life and helping others.

Reward: You will have more resources to use as a powerful tool to accomplish greater things. You will succeed better through ethical ways, rather than through greed or manipulation.

Affirmation: "I will be a good resource manager by acquiring money through diligent labor, and creative resourcefulness, while not neglecting my responsibilities!"

"I" TYPE RESOURCE MANAGERS

In A Word: Impulsive – "How fast can I get money?"

Abilities: They make working fun. There is never a dull moment when they are on the job. They are creative in acquiring more resources. High energy and wanting to work in front of others is their work identity.

Strategies: Being willing to help others succeed on their job and they will help you succeed on your job. Stay on task and be willing to work outside the spotlight. Concentrate on doing one thing well. Be honest in your presentations.

Warning: Guard against get-rich-quick opportunities. Research and wait before committing to any financial investment. Be consistent in doing one job well before moving on to the next task. Remember getting money is as much, if not more important than spending money.

Reward: You will have more financial resources when you avoid get-rich-quick schemes. By staying focused on doing one project well, you will be respected by your colleagues and others.

Affirmation: "I will remain focused staying on task, doing my job well, while talking less and working diligently."

"S" TYPE RESOURCE MANAGERS

In A Word: Steady – "Stay on course!"

Abilities: They are steady workers. They work well with others. Stays focused on one stream of income that is working well. Sensitive to change in financial market.

Strategies: Become more pro-active in seeking better employment or investment opportunities. Be more confident and assertive in asking for a salary increase. Look for more creative ways to increase your finances.

Warning: Do not let people manipulate you in using improper business ethics to acquire funds. Do not wait too long to decide on taking advantage of a new and proven way to increase your income. Be more creative for ways to add to your finances, continue to be alert for more opportunities to do so.

Reward: You are a steady worker, so more income will come your way. Remember to share with other how you succeeded!

Affirmation: "I will be willing to attempt new ways to increase my income so I can provide more for my present and future well-being!"

"C" TYPE RESOURCE MANAGERS

In A Word: Calculating – "What's the best deal!"

Abilities: They are very careful in getting their finances without compromising their personal values. They will spend time researching how to get the most "bang for their buck."

Strategies: Make quicker decisions so the financial opportunity is not lost. Involve more people in your investment strategies. Communicate with your family the what, when, where, who, why, and how you get your resources. Look for multiple streams of income.

Warning: Do not get discouraged by the impulsive way others try to get money. Do not spend too much time analyzing every investment opportunity. Remember the importance of optimism and faith.

Reward: You will experience joy and satisfaction for the basic needs of life. When you work together with others on your team, you will get more done and increase income.

Affirmation: "I will stop worrying about my finances and be more positive about my future. After I calculate the best way to increase my income, I will work joyfully and diligently with a good attitude."

How DISC Personality Types GUARD Their Money

Guarding and protecting your money is so important in today's economy. Many unknown factors affect our savings and investments. Wise managers of their finances will pay close attention to how they guard their money.

"D" TYPE RESOURCE MANAGERS

In A Word: Determined – "This is how it is done."

Abilities: Having resources to do things is important to them. They are determined to get the very best deal. It is easy for them to say "no" to telemarketers and pushy sales people. They want to control how their money is guarded and given away.

Strategies: Take time to do research before spending your money. Pay bills promptly. Keep records. Think more before proceeding with major expenses.

Warning: Remember the difference between hoarding and saving your money. Stay within a budget. Prioritize your spending. Guarding your money is to be balanced with wisely using your resources to add value to others.

Reward: You will have the satisfaction of having the resources to bless your family and others. More money will be available to help others.

Affirmation: "I will manage my resources more wisely and help others with my bounty, rather than always wanting to get more!"

"I" TYPE RESOURCE MANAGERS

In A Word: Impressive – "It must look good!"

Abilities: Leaves a good impression. Knows how to "look good." Inspires others with what they have. Stylish. Communicates well and is very positive. Can find the silver lining in every cloud.

Strategies: Guard against emotional and impulsive spending. Control your entertainment, fashions, and grooming / personal care expenses. Look for the best buy.

Warning: Do not spend money you do not have. Bigger is not necessarily better. Use a budget. Pay bills on time. Build sales resistance. Avoid cosigning. Do not try to "buy friends."

Reward: You will have more in savings. You will be identified as a person of sound money management. People will seek you out for financial counsel.

Affirmation: "I will use my resources *not* to impress people but to be a responsible person. I will guard my optimism against "getting rich quick" for my own vain glory!"

"S" TYPE RESOURCE MANAGERS

In A Word: "Money is safe with them."

Abilities: They are more security-minded with money. Safety and stability are important to where their money is kept. Bills are paid promptly.

Strategies: Say "no" sooner to telemarketers and pushy sales people. Start saving today. Do no accept the first offer for interest on your savings. Shop around.

Warning: Do not wait to begin a money management system. Do not let people manipulate you in spending money.

Reward: You will have money when others will not. Others will come to you for financial advice.

Affirmation: "I will guard my resources so I have more to invest and with which to help others!"

"C" TYPE RESOURCE MANAGERS

In A Word: "Capable money-managers!"

Abilities: Contemplative, "savers," find the best deals, stretch the dollar to get the most mileage, good spending controls.

Strategies: Be more generous and thoughtful with your finances. Use a budget and record keeping as a guideline not a law.

Warning: Do not be stingy. Do not judge others on how they spend or use money.

Reward: You will be appreciated when you are generous. You will be recognized as a person who cares about people, not how much money you saved.

Affirmation: "I will be more liberal with my finances, and share what I have earned with those individuals and organizations that are truly needy."

How DISC Personality Types GIVE Their Money

Sharing your income should be a vital part of your financial plan. Life works best when it is balanced. Giving is just as important as receiving.

"D" TYPE RESOURCE MANAGERS

In A Word: Direct – "Give it NOW (often with strings attached)!"

Abilities: Decisiveness, purposeful, give to get a task done, generous, serious about financial matters.

Strategies: Do research before you give. Give to people not just tasks or organizations. Look for people in need.

Warning: Do not give money and resources to control people. Be flexible in how you give. Think before donating. Follow through on any promise commitments you make.

Reward: You will make a good financial counselor. You also have a unique ability to "make" money. You accomplish great things when you give.

Affirmation: "I will be generous with my money even when I can not control how it is used!"

"I" TYPE RESOURCE MANAGERS

In A Word: Influencing – "Enthusiastic in making a difference!"

Abilities: Cheerful givers, liberal and free with their finances, generous, quick to give, optimistic, impressive.

Strategies: Think before writing a check. Give secretly. Have a strategy in your giving rather than being impulsive. Be consistent in your giving.

Warning: Do not be proud of all you give. Have a giving-plan. Give to meet the needs of a project, not only to a person's need.

Reward: Accomplish more when you control how much you talk about giving and actually do give. Others will be encouraged to give by your enthusiasm about financial management.

Affirmation: "I will not give my money to impress people and tell others about my giving!"

"S" TYPE RESOURCE MANAGERS

In A Word: Sensitive – "Who needs financial help?"

Abilities: Sensitive to the needs of others, submissive (willing) givers, secret in their giving, sacrificial. Able to see the little things that need financial help.

Strategies: Guard your sincere desire to give with a stronger determination to do what is right. Be creative and innovative with how you give.

Warning: Do not wait to give when an opportunity arises. But also do not be taken advantage of with every appeal. Keep your giving within your budget.

Reward: You are a stable financial giver who avoids financial disasters. You will often be sought out for help and are respected for your sacrificial giving.

Affirmation: "I will balance my giving between spontaneous and strategic giving!"

"C" TYPE RESOURCE MANAGERS

In A Word: Careful – "Strategic givers!"

Abilities: Cautious, compliant, calculating in what the real needs are before they give. They are consistent and private when they give, usually gives to projects.

Strategies: Balance giving between project and people needs. Use your competence in giving to help others learn how to give. Work on positive solutions to solve financial problems.

Warning: Do not get discouraged by the giving strategies of others. Remember you are really giving to help others, regardless of what they do with your gifts.

Reward: You make a great financial giving planner. You will be more appreciated when you give more spontaneously.

Affirmation: "I will give cheerfully and spontaneously to the needs of others even when I don't think they deserve it."

Improving Time Management

The following are simple insights to help you improve your time-management skills from your personality perspective. Focus on your primary and secondary types. Also study this entire section to learn more about how all 4 DISC personality types relate to time-management. These insights are designed to help you and others recognize how being good managers of the time given us is an essential part of our lives.

"D" TYPE RESOURCE MANAGERS

In A Word: Direct — "Do it NOW!"

Abilities: Getting things done, leading, taking a stand, confronting issues, persevering, dictating, making decisions and control.

Strategies: Plan your work and work your plan. See the "little things" as well as the big picture. Seek counsel along the way. Slow down. Write out your long and short term goals.

Warning: Do not push ahead without counting the cost first. Learn to rest along the way. Do not sacrifice your family and church while working so hard. Do not try to cram too much into your schedule. Remember, you need others to get the job done.

Reward: You will get more done by delegating tasks. Your health, family, and faith will be blessed. Your results will be more gold, silver, and precious stones, rather than wood, hay, and stubble.

Affirmation: "I will prioritize my time to do what I need to do for my family and others first!"

"I" TYPE RESOURCE MANAGERS

In A Word: Inspirational — "Time is short. Let's have fun!"

Abilities: Spontaneous, communicating, inspiring, influencing, making friends, optimistic, enthusiastic.

Strategies: Think before committing to anything. Write out your daily schedule of things to do. Concentrate on the behind the scenes that often are neglected. Plan with tomorrow in mind.

Warning: Use your persuasive personality to encourage people without manipulating them. Do not be proud of all you get done. Do not seek to be recognized for what you do. Do not waste time talking so much or wanting to be around people a lot.

Reward: Accomplish so much more when you control your talking to people and getting your work done behind the scenes. You will be recognized as a balanced person who can communicate well, but also can do what needs to be done by yourself.

Affirmation:" I will talk less and be a better listener, while focusing on people and tasks the same."

"S" TYPE RESOURCE MANAGERS

In A Word: Relational — "Slow plodders you can count on!"

Abilities: Supporting, serving, finishing what others start, working behind scenes, doing what needs done in their time.

Strategies: Be more assertive. Take charge when things or people seem uncertain. Be more confident. See the big picture also and look beyond the small steps along the way. Set time limits on yourself and others to get things done. Do not procrastinate or put off what needs to be done.

Warning: Do not waste your time with people who just want to talk. Do not let people side-track you or manipulate you in to doing things that are not imperative. Be kind, but not too kind.

Reward: Believe that you can do anything you set your mind and will to do. Step out and try the difficult. You may be surprised what you can do!

Affirmation: "I will be stronger and more assertive even when I don't feel capable of doing something!"

"C" TYPE RESOURCE MANAGERS

In A Word: Organized — "Meticulous planners!"

Abilities: Analyzing, improving, discerning, calculating, following directions, doing the right things.

Strategies: Work on positive ways to get others involved in tasks. Relax your schedule and look at the bright side more. Involve more people in plans. Communicate your plans in short and simple instructions. Focus on the absolute necessities first. Articulate your plans with enthusiasm and grace.

Warning: Do not get discouraged by the disorganization of others. Do not spend too much time thinking about everything that needs to be done. Do not over analyze everything. Get others involved and do not try to do everything yourself.

Reward: More satisfaction of getting jobs done without being frustrated. Getting more done with little time. Getting people to work with you more, because the "atmosphere" is better.

Affirmation: "I will be more optimistic in the midst of problems and not get bogged down in the details."

Balancing Your Time

As good stewards in life, time becomes our friend or foe. It will either work for us or against us. To use our time wisely, we must properly balance it. Everyone is given the same amount of time each day. We either waste it or use it. We must recognize how important time is for ourselves and others. Neglecting our families, worship, and helping others will greatly affect the results of how we use our time.

Someone has said, "The only excuse for activity is results!" All our activity during each day should be evaluated in light of results. Some results can be clearly seen, while other results will only be seen by eternal values. Balancing our measurable results with our results unseen by others can be very difficult.

Doing "things" is not always best. Learning how to be "still and waiting" can be just as important. The key to balancing our time-management challenges is setting aside time for those things that are temporal and those things that are eternal.

"D" Types

Your active / task-oriented life style makes you a determined, doer and driver type. You need to slow down and make time work for you. You are often "too busy" to take care of the more "important" things in life, such as your family, worship, and community service. Ask five of your best friends and / or close family members if they think you work too hard.

Think it over:
- Do I control my natural drive to work hard?
- Have I determined to take care of the little things?

- Do I discipline my time and energy?
- Have I learned how to stop and be more careful?
- Do I believe that if I am too busy for others, I'm just too busy?
- Do I spend my time building deep relationships?

"I" Types

Influencing types are often the most challenged by time. They tend to be the most sociable and friendly. Talking and being around people is very important to them. Lots of time is often wasted in "chit-chat" and endless conversations about nothing. They are the most encouraging to be around, but often neglect their duties and responsibilities time-wise.

Think it over:

- Do I recognize how much I talk to others and waste a lot of time?
- Do I excuse my lack of discipline concerning getting tasks done on time because so many people like me?
- Am I always in a rush because I do not plan ahead or often get distracted?

"S" Types

Submissive types are often the most dependable, but also controlled by others. They do not like to say, "No" and disappoint people. Concerned with safe and secure relationships, they tend to be too nice and kind. Spending time with someone just to listen to all their problems or an exciting opportunity makes them vulnerable to those who will take advantage of them.

Think it over:

- Do I let people use and control me?
- Do I recognize that my kindness can often become a source of wasting time?
- Do I procrastinate doing important tasks that can be put off until later?
- Do I need to be more aggressive and assertive?

"C" Types

Cautious and compliant types are often the most time-conscious, but they can be too regimented. They can be too organized and picky without much flexibility. They need to learn how to relax and take it easier in life. They are methodical and analytical, but should not let urgency take the place of those things that are eternal. They are organized and efficient when it comes to tasks, but they often come across as cold.

Think it over:

- Do you let the little details bother you?
- Have you earned the reputation of being a "picky perfectionist" in a bad sense?
- Do people respect your opinions or ever criticize, "why do you always have to be right?"
- How are you learning to be more flexible?
- Can I make quicker decisions?

Now What About Your Time?

Dr. Mark Cambron often said, "Time is an island in the sea of God's eternity. It begins with man and ends with man." This is so simple, yet profound. Time is only human. It was designed for humankind to use and not abuse. How we use our time will be a reflection on what we think about and what we value most in life.

There are five major areas where we should spend most of our time — with our (1) faith, (2) family, (3) work, (4) others and (5) self. We need to be wise time-managers of each of these areas. Abusing these areas will violate the universal plan for our lives. We were created with purpose. We were given the element of time to live by faith, so we must take a serious look at what we do with our time!

The way we spend our time as a wise steward is so important. Spending time with our families is especially vital. An ancient proverb says, "If you don't provide (time) for your own, you're less than an infidel." Work is one of those necessary time requirements. "You don't work, you don't eat." Making time for others in our community and throughout the world is also necessary. Finally, we need to save time for ourselves. This does not mean that we only give ourselves whatever time is leftover. We should balance our time in all five areas.

The following are practical insights that will help all DISC personality types improve their use of time. The biggest challenge is that time does not stand still and we can never get it back. We must use our time wisely.

Be healthy, wealthy, and wise by controlling your motivations!

"D" Types and Time For:

Faith: Be **DEDICATED** to your faith! Set aside a specific time each day to strengthen your faith.

Family: Be **DECISIVE** and do not get distracted with other "important" things to do.

Work: Be **DILIGENT** and work hard. You may be the closest influence others will ever see.

Others: Be **DETERMINED** to help others by giving them your time and assistance.

Self: Be **DEMANDING** of yourself and do not let your feelings influence you to take time for everything else and not for yourself.

"I" Types and Time For:

Faith: Be **INSPIRED** and take time each day to share the love and forgiveness of your faith with others.

Family: Be **INFLUENCING** as an example to your family in word and in deed (not just your talk, but also with your walk).

Work: Be **INDUSTRIOUS,** working harder and talking less so your employer and fellow employees will learn from your example.

Be healthy, wealthy, and wise by controlling your motivations!

Others: Be **IMPRESSIVE** by placing others above yourself. Do not be self-centered or egotistical. Talk less and listen more.

Self: Be **IMAGINATIVE** and find ways to help yourself, rather than pleasing everyone else.

"S" Types and Time For:

Faith: Be **SUBMISSIVE** to your faith first, giving it the time and attention entrusted to you.

Family: Be **SWEET** and loving. Love is often spelled: "T-I-M-E" when it comes to your family.

Work: Be **STRONGER** and assertive. People will be impressed by how much you get done with so little time.

Others: Be **SENSITIVE** to the needs of others, but do not let them always take advantage of you. "NO" is also okay to say.

Self: Be **STRONG** and do not let people "steal" your time by expecting you to constantly listen to them or convince you to do something for them that you really do not have time to do.

"C" Types and Time For:

Faith: Be **CAREFUL** to not neglect your faith because of all the other things you need to do each day.

Family: Be **CONSISTENT** and show your family they are also serious priority in your life.

Work: Be **CONSCIENTIOUS**, not contentious. Do your work well without criticizing or condemning the labor of others.

Others: Be **COURTEOUS** and recognize the value of other people's opinions and contributions.

Self: Be **CARING** of yourself. There is nothing wrong with spending time on yourself. Do something relaxing.

How you manage your health, time and money are the direct results of how you govern your personality. You can win life's everyday challenges by understanding how you are wired, and how your motivations affect you. When you come to the end of life's road, only a few things are going to really matter.

Some of your thoughts will focus on your family and friends. Another interest will be your faith and future. Your greatest regrets or blessings will come from how you took care of your body, spent your time, and managed your money.

Do not wait to seriously consider how you are using one of your most valuable resources — your own personality. It is not your total being, because you are also a physical, emotional, intellectual, and spiritual being. However, it is part of the core within you.

You were created by intelligent design to experience more than you can ever imagined. Discover your purpose. Begin each day by acknowledging your affirmation to control your personality, rather than letting it control you.

Conclusion

How should I conclude something that seems to never end? Every day I learn new insights about why people do what they do. Being an observer of human behavior can be fascinating. Just sit a while in a mall and watch people as they pass by.

You should be able to observe the "D"s as they hurry along on their serious missions. Look for the "I"s as they are the center of attention, laughing and talking. The "S"s will often be the quiet and polite ones. And the "C"s will look intense and focused.

Regardless of how you can identify others, stop and think about how people see you. Can you adapt and are you flexible? Can you become something you are not, for the sake of others? Or do you think that everything revolves around you?

Does everyone have to accept you "just the way you are?" Are you thinking right now, "so what's wrong with that?" If you want to be effective and successful, you must accept the fact that everything does not revolve around you. Life is full of compromises. You have to be flexible and responsive to the needs of others first.

When you do, it will come back to benefit you. There is a ancient proverb that says, "You reap what you sow!" Invest in blessing others and you will be blessed. Control your personality and motivations, rather than expecting others to control theirs for your sake. You only have to answer for what you do.

Have you gotten the point yet? If not, here it is.

The Main Point

Simply put, the main point of all this is recognizing if you are a high "D," that the "D" in you may cause you to explode under pressure. Or if you are a low "D," you may allow people to control you, often forcing you to weaken under pressure.

If you are a high "I," you may find yourself exaggerating, being emotional, and talking too much. Or if you are a low "I," you may let people do all the talking and not share in the conversation.

If you are a high "S," you may allow yourself to be intimidated or manipulated. Or if you are a low "S," you may not care enough about what others feel and be too secure in yourself.

If you are a high "C," you may worry a lot or be "too concerned" about most things. Or if you are a low "C," you may not think or consider enough about the little things that really matter.

I may be over-simplifying all this, but it is important that you stop and think about it. There is an ancient saying, "Selah," which means "pause and consider" or "stop and think." That comes easy for "S"s and "C"s, but you "D"s and "I"s must also "Selah."

Always keep in mind that most people are blends, with two or three types comprising their personality. Do not jump to conclusions or pigeonhole people. Simply observe, try to identify, and respond to people based on their personality needs and interests.

There are more important lessons to learn and letters to remember, than just the DISC letters. On a lighter side, a while back I read some "deep" insights from the great philosopher Dr. Seuss, "On Beyond Zebra." I do not remember exactly how it went, but I tried memorizing it and came out with the following paraphrase.

On Beyond Z

"Said, Conrad Cornelius O'Donal Odel, my very young friend who was learning to spell, 'A is for ape, B is for bear, C is for camel, H is for hair, M is for mouse, R is for rat, and I know all twenty-six letters like that.

Through Z is for Zebra, I know them all well,' said Conrad Cornelius O'Donal Odel.

Then he almost fell flat on his face on the floor when I picked up a chalk and drew one letter more. A letter he never dreamed of before.

And I said, 'You can stop with the letter Z. A lot of people stop with a Z, but not me. There are places I go and places I see I could never spell if I stopped with a Z.

I'm telling you this because you're one of my friends. My alphabet starts where your alphabet ends. My alphabet starts with the letter called Uz. It's the letter I use to spell Uzamatuz.

So on beyond Z!

Explore like Columbus. Discover new letters like Wum, which is for Wumpish.

My high sounding whale who never comes up until it's time to refill. It's high time you were shown, you really don't know all there is to be known.'"

Dr. Seuss had some great insights we should all consider. May I add, there are more important letters than DISC. How about considering the letters "OTHERS?"

We need to focus on those things that are beyond ourselves and our personalities. We should focus on helping others by controlling our personalities, rather than expecting them to control their temperaments. We must focus on being supernatural, rather than the natural. We should seek to be the person or personality that others need around them to help them, instead of expecting them to meet our needs, fulfilling our strengths or uniqueness.

People will then learn the answer when they ask:

"So, you're unique! What's your point?"

So, You're Unique!
What's Your Point?

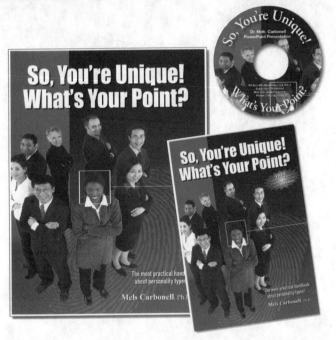

"PEP" Personal Enrichment Pac

1 — "So, You're Unique! What's Your Point?" Textbook
1 — "SYU" Life Planner Notebook (over 130 pages)
1 — "SYU" PowerPoint Presentation (over 400 slides)
1 — Professionals / Leaders Online Profile (nearly 100 pages)

Masters Institute

Conference Calls (8 weeks —1 1/2 hours each week) Training Course

- Become Executive / Masters Certified!
- Receive Highest Level of Certification!
- Become Licensed to Teach Course!
- Receive Maximum Discounts!

For more info, call: (706) 492-5490   *Web site: www.UniquelyYou.com*

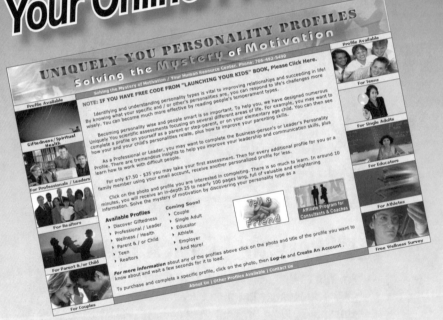

Three Ways

Uniquely You Human Resources Can Help You!

1

Uniquely You Online Certification Training

Become a Certified Trainer or Coach for groups, businesses, and/or schools!

- Certified Church Health Diagnostic Spec. (CHDS)
- Certified Leadership Training Specialist (CLTS)
- Certified Wellness Dynamics Specialist (CWDS)
- Certified Human Relations Specialist (CHRS)
- Certified Human Behavior Consultant (CHBC)
- Certified Church Assimilation Specialist (CCAS)

Learn How To Increase Involvement & Reduce Conflicts from the convenience of your phone and computer!

1, 2, or 3 Day Onsite Certification Training

Basic, Specialist, and Advanced Training now available

Over 1,000,000 profiles now in print!

2

Sponsor a Discover Your Giftedness Seminar at no cost to your group's budget!

Help your members get involved in the activites and responsibilies of your group by identifying their giftedness. Uniquely You will pay for all travel, lodging, materials, and honorariums if your group will simply promote and register a guaranteed number of people to attend the seminar.

Oak Cliff Bible Fellowship — Dr. Tony Evans Pastor

Presenters: Dr. Mels Carbonell, Dr. Stan Ponz, or one of their Certified Trainers

Rick Warren, Pastor	Zig Ziglar, Author
Saddleback Church	"Dr. Mels Carbonell
"One of the best seminars ever!"	has a message America needs to hear!"

3

Masters Institute Coaching Conference Calls

Mels Carbonell Ph.D.   Stan Ponz D.Min.

Receive personal coaching and consulting on various leadership, team building, health, and professional issues that will make a difference. This 10 weeks (1 1/2 hour sessions) conference call course will use Dr. Carbonell's newest book, *"So, you're unique! What's your point?* as the text book, along with PowerPoint presentations and Action Plans. Once you complete this course you will be Certified as an *Executive Trainer and Affiliate,* the highest training and best discounts on recourses offered.

For more info, call: (706) 492-5490

Web site: www.UniquelyYou.NET

Professionals Personality Profile

25 pages

This profile is designed specifically to use for business and management purposes.

It is perfect for Staff Development, Team Building, Leadership Training, Interviewing Prospective Staff, Sales and Customer Service Training, plus it is a powerful tool to reach business-people in the Marketplace.

Features:
- Uniquely You Questionnaire
- Interpretation of DISC Graphs
- Understanding The Two Graphs
- How To Read The DISC Graphs
- Discovering Your Behavioral Blends
- Controlling Your Behavioral Blends
- Practical Application / Stress Management
- Leadership Insights
- Job/Profile Indicator
- Job Intensity Factors
- Interview Questions / Personal Insights
- Team Building Reflections
- Team Dynamics
- Intensity Insights • Action Plan
- Sales Insights • Servicing Styles
- Dealing With Objections
- First Signs / Prospecting

Wellness Dyanmics (DISC) Personality Profile

This profile is specifically designed to help everyone identify (DISC) motivations in order to improve health and wellness.

Features:
- Why Wellness?
- Uniquely You Questionnaire
- Instructions to complete profile
- Interpretation of DISC Personality Types
- Discovering Your Behavioral Blends
- How To Read The DISC Graphs
- Personality Questionnaire
- Identify 4 DISC Temperament Types
- Discovering Behavioral Blends
- Practical Application
- Stress Management
- How DISC Personality Types Respond To Attitude, Diet, Exercise, & Nutrition
- To Your Health & Balancing Your Health
- Problems & Suggested Solutions
- Now What?

Ideal for:
- Personal Development
- Staff Training
- Communications Skills
- Leadership Training
- Coaching & Consulting

19 pages

The Professionals Profile can also be completed online. It is the "most comprehensive and practical profile available" with nearly 100 pages.

Go to:
www.UniquelyYou.NET
or phone:
(706) 492-5490
for more info.

For **FREE** Wellness Survey and Personality Profile go to:
www.WellnessDynamics.com

Affiliate Programs
Receive Discounts or Earn Commissions!

Receive discounts or commissions by placing our online profile link on your web site or someone else's site. This is a great opportunity for businesses, churches and organizations to offer their members or customers any of our profiles online 24/7, plus to complete in the convenience of their own homes or offices.

Become a Partner and receive substantial discounts!

For example, if you as an organization, church, business owner or leader want your members, staff, or customers to complete one of our profiles and receive a discount, you can become a *Partner*.

Simply place our:

www.uniquelyyou.NET

link on your web Home Page and receive an instant discount for everyone who completes his or her profile through your site.

Become an Affiliate and receive unlimited commissions!

Uniquely You Profiler

Affiliation Program

Ground Floor Opportunity!

If you or your organization becomes one of our *Affiliates Masters*, you can receive commissions. *Basic, Specialist, Advanced, and Executive Certified* individuals will continue to receive their discounts for themselves or their organization's phone-in orders.

Affiliates that build a downline with customers who also want to become *Affiliates* can do so

The BEST Commissions and Consulting Offer Available!

You can receive commissions for every First Level profile purchased at the current $7.50 or $35 retail price.

This is a phenomenal offer!

Become a Partner and save, save, save!
Become an Affiliate and earn, earn, earn!

Uniquely You is committed to providing the best human behavioral and biblical resources available, plus helping its consultants and customers do their best!

Affiliate Program Details Are Tentitive.
Final figures will be posted on our web site at:
www.UniquelyYou.NET

SPONSOR A SEMINAR FOR YOUR GROUP

If you have never attended one of our Uniquely You seminars, you owe it to yourself to view our website and take a look at our current seminar schedule (www.myuy.com), or better yet, schedule one of your own! That's Right! You can host a Uniquely You seminar for your group, at no cost. The people who attend pay an individual fee.

Call 1-706-492-5490 for further information.

Uniquely You™ Resources
PO Box 490
Blue Ridge, GA 30513
e-mail: drmels@myuy.com
706-492-5490